Sweet Synchronicity: Finding Annie Besant, Discovering Krishnamurti

Elizabeth Spring, M.A.

ISBN-13 978-069-2326268
ISBN-10 069-232626X
Archeon Press
To order additional copies:
www.elizabethspring.com
www.amazon.com

Dedication

~To you, the Reader~

"Tis the good reader that makes the good book; in every book he finds passages which seem to be confidences or asides hidden from all else and unmistakably meant for his ear; the profit of books is according to the sensibility of the reader; the profoundest thought or passion sleeps as in a mine, until it is discovered by an equal mind and heart."
Ralph Waldo Emerson

This book is based on the lives of Annie Besant, J, Krishnamurti, and the author, Elizabeth Spring. Although the basis of the story is true as told, there are some changes that modify the story to put it into a literary form. There are also disagreements over the nature of some of the people and events as noted in conflicting histories. I trust the reader will understand that this book represents my personal experience and many years spent in research.

Annie Besant

Table of Contents

One

Finding Annie

It was a crisp October day in the upscale bucolic village of Litchfield, Connecticut. I was visiting my seventy year old mother, when on an 'afternoon outing' we stumbled upon the kind of bookstore that barely exists anymore. Wooden beams framed the small cluttered interior of the room overflowing with books and a woodstove warmed the chilled air. I felt excited; maybe there would be something here for me.

I would have checked out the astrology section first, but instead bumped into a table, over which hovered a curious sign: "People Forgotten in History," and there she was—a woman staring from the cover of a book directly into my eyes. It was a slim book with the simple title of *Annie Besant* followed by the subtitle: *Passionate campaigner for social and political rights, seeker after spiritual truth, and a woman of extraordinary personal courage.* I looked at her face—young, earnest, intense, with dark eyes set between high cheekbones and framed with short curly brown hair. But it was her direct stare that defied any attempt to return her to the slush pile of books on the table.

So *"Annie"* came home with me that day, and after dinner, I returned to my childhood bedroom and began to read. It wasn't until dawn that I finally put the book down; finished and mesmerized. Her story captured me, not just her struggles and defeats, but something about who she was—was so like me—although her life was so large and mine so small. Could this be just co-incidence and serendipity? It felt as if there was a sweet synchronicity resonating between us.

That next morning my words were a torrent of jagged emotion as I tried to tell my mother about Annie: "When Annie was young she was a minister's wife in a poverty-stricken area of England where she anguished over the appalling conditions and pain she saw—she felt that what women needed was *to not* have a life of continuous child-bearing—she felt they needed to know about birth control. So she found a booklet on contraception—in 1875—and gave it out to everyone—lots of people! She had it printed and distributed all over England—and it so enraged her husband that he brought her to trial where the courts declared her an *unfit mother* for corrupting the morals of the young. Can you *believe it?*" I caught my breath.

Mother was busily spreading butter on her toast. Without saying a word she got up and walked to the kitchen to get more coffee.

"They took her children away from her!" My voice hovered between a scream and a plea for understanding. I took a deep breath and lowered my voice to a rational level. "And after that she led the match girls in a strike in London that changed everything for them—they were being poisoned by match chemicals, working 10 hours a day for a pittance!"

No comment. I wrapped my hands, tightening my grip, around the chipped coffee mug I had long ago made for her. She poured me more coffee.

Mother sat down and raised her eyelids. "Life is cruel, but what can we do? Were you reading all night? That's not good for you honey, and now you've got to go back and leave me here, again." She sighed. I felt the usual twang of guilt, but this time it was layered with a hopeless anger that we would never connect. Mother always felt abandoned when I left her home in Connecticut for Rhode Island.

Returning home to Newport, I made straight away for the Redwood Library on Bellevue Avenue. Here in this private old library there must be some dusty volume on the life of Annie Besant. I inquired; there was indeed such a book; the librarian handed me a faded red tome called "The Passionate Pilgrim."

Opening this hard-covered book I saw that it hadn't been signed out of the library for over 15 years—but—there on the inside cover of the book was her full birth chart! I gasped. Annie was born on Oct. 1st 1847 at 5:39 pm, and I was born Oct 1st 1947, at 5:34 pm —the same day, exactly 100 years and 5 minutes apart. We were both Libras with Aries rising, and many aspects in our charts were similar. A shiver went through me.

As I read this second book I found out that Annie was ¾ Irish, same as me, but she was born in England whereas I was born in New England. Annie was born Annie Wood, and I was born Janet Fenn. In marriage she changed her name from Wood to Besant, and I changed from Fenn to Spring. When I was forty, I took my grandmother's first name, Elizabeth. I never felt that I was a "Janet", but I felt close to my grandmother and loved her name, so I changed it—but surely this wasn't good daughterly etiquette.

I was a wife and mother like Annie—I was a woman with a strong Irish temperament that came out in passionate "Letters to the Editor" and in marches for Civil Rights and the Equal Rights Amendment. I was not too different from many people of my generation, but Annie was a much more outrageous public woman in her time—she was consistently on the front page of the *London Times* for her aggravating attacks on British society—how dare she challenge their sex lives with birth control information and their businesses with labor strikes for women? How dare she challenge the morality of the British hold on India, ultimately taking sides with the Indians till she became President of their National Congress? And most outrageous of all, how dare she adopt a sickly Indian boy, Krishnamurti, and raise him to become what the newspapers called him to be—a "Messiah."

Why had I never heard of this woman who challenged history in England and India? Was her story simply too outrageous for people to follow past her early social reforming years in London? Annie's life as a radical reformer was understandable, in fact, the British Broadcasting Corporation created a television series on her life that ended with those radical years in England—but they stopped telling the story of her life when she became forty years old! Was the second half of her life neglected or erased because it was too hard for most people to understand? I think so.

My life would change radically when I was around the age of forty, the same age as Annie was when she wrote her autobiography; something many people do towards the end of their life, not the middle. But there was a radical break in her life at that point, and in her autobiography she began with a reflection on her horoscope, and a small digression on the value of astrology.

Being an astrologer myself I knew two things: one, that even mentioning astrology was unusual for a woman who was born in 1847 and died in 1933—unusual because astrology wasn't at all popular or accepted then, and two, that around the age of forty is the astrological time of what is called the "Uranus Opposition," a time when most people make radical life changes. So it was not unusual for a change to occur in both of us then, but more interesting that we both became increasingly fascinated by astrology and spirituality at that same point.

I pored over Annie's chart and my own. I'm a professional astrologer who accepts the influences of reincarnation on the chart and the theories of Carl Jung, particularly on synchronicity or "meaningful co-incidences." As I looked at the charts I noticed there were differences, but many similarities, aside from the fact that we were both Libras. My astrological "niche" is about the North and South Nodes in the birth chart—these are the places where the re-incarnational life story and life lessons interact and this is where I caught my breath again—Annie's North Node pierced through my Sun like an arrow.

Let me explain a little to those who may be interested in astrology: I recently wrote a book called: *North Node Astrology; Rediscovering Your Life Direction and Soul Purpose.* The North Node, like a *North Star,* guides us to where the Soul wants to go, and the experiences it wants to have or move towards, while the South Node represents what we want to move away from: our old karmic patterns best left behind.

What was most compelling about comparing our charts was that we appeared to have a soul connection regardless of the time we each lived in and regardless of the outer facts of our lives. Annie's North Node, the direction where the Soul wants to move towards, conjoined or pierced my Libra Sun sign, meaning that something about who I am might echo a soul-wish of hers. It could be as simple as having a simpler more peaceful life, because I have my North Node in the Sign that longs for serenity: Taurus. Her South Node, reflective of the past and past lives, lodged itself right on my Aries Rising Sign, pointing to problems we both have faced, including indignation at social injustices. With Aries Rising there's a tendency to be a "spiritual warrior."

And if we want to think *bizarre*, my Moon, representing something of my maternal and emotional experience, aligns perfectly with Annie's Pluto, the Lord of the Underworld. Pluto is the planet representing death, rebirth, and "life on the other side." Maybe it's not that strange then that I'm trying to reach a woman who's "on the other side?"

So it was the Nodal aspects of the charts that pointed to something unusual: if I were talking to a client about the comparison of these two charts with these particular aspects, I would tell them that there was a very good chance these two people had some kind of connection via reincarnation. But what that connection was, wasn't exactly clear. Were these similar life lessons, or was there a previous life connection, or had one Soul actually been born again in the other?

Also in comparing the two charts, I saw that Annie and I had some of the usual heart-aching problems with mothers—the Moon representing the Mother in a chart. Annie had her Moon in the maternal sign of Cancer in a tense square to unpredictable Uranus, and I had my Moon in Aries in a tense square to assertive Mars. Annie's life with her mother was a source of great pain, while my maternal relationship was abusive at times. All of this was interesting to contemplate at the time, but what was I to do with it? This isn't an astrology book, but in the very last chapter I'll share more observations with the reader about the charts.

I finished the last page of the old red book and sat staring out the bay window. Harry walked in the back door from the pottery studio. "What's happening, Sweetie?"

I attempted a smile. He walked over and ruffled my dishelved hair which I tried to keep up in a proper bun on top of my head. My dark blond hair was getting too long and yet I loved that old fashioned look, it seemed to fit me. I must have looked very serious. "Come have a glass of wine, honey, you've got to put those books away."

He pulled up a chair and poured two glasses while I stared out the window. "So? Out with it, my dear—what's wrong?" After fourteen years of marriage he knew when I was in a mood. The blood rushed to my cheeks. I gave his hand a squeeze then picked up the little book I'd bought that first day I found Annie and handed it to him.

He took it out of my hands and with a mocking grand gesture read a section of the back cover: "Annie Besant grew into becoming what George Bernard Shaw called 'the greatest orator of the century' as well as his financial supporter and mentor. When she traveled across America in 1922 she often spoke to packed theatre houses and auditoriums six nights a week and was frequently paid a thousand dollars a night."

"Wow, she was quite a superstar back then." Harry's eyebrows lifted.

"Keep reading" I whispered.

"In 1889, at the age of 41, she shocked the world when she became a devoted supporter of the Russian psychic, Madame Helena Blavatsky—and on Blavatsky's death two years later Annie became president of the world's largest occult religion, Theosophy. Although Annie was always committed to social betterment, it was the search for life's meaning and spiritual Truth which was the most consistent thread running through her life. At the age of sixty her political activism resurfaced, and after years of inciting the Indians for home rule for India, Annie became, at the age of seventy, the President of India's National Congress, just before Gandhi."

"Can you believe this? One woman....?" he said, looking up at me surprised. My eyes must have looked like shiny dark pools. I had lost so much sleep. "But still, why are you in this... state? Was your mother--?"

I shook my head and grabbed the book again: "Listen to this: her most outrageous act was when she presented to the world, her adopted son, J. Krishnamurti, as a Spiritual Teacher—a young Indian boy the newspapers called *The Young Messiah*." I threw the book down. "These wealthy British Theosophists groomed him to be the second coming of Christ!" I picked up the book again and opened it to newspaper photos of Annie with Krishnamurti on her arm: *Young Messiah to come to America.* "Look here—this was in 1927. She must have really seen something—extraordinary—in him!"

I took a sip of wine and went on: "So Annie, and thousands of people, actually believed that this very quiet boy, whom they had raised like an English Brahmin to be a

Star—to be a Guru— would be the Avatar for the New Age, the one Madame Blavatsky predicted would come….and you know what he did?"

Harry leaned toward me, looking on the edge of confusion. "No—this is unbelievable. This is true?"

"All true." I gulped down some wine and continued: "Well—first this boy just about had a nervous breakdown—no, he *did* have a nervous breakdown around the age of thirty-three, and then he stood up one day in Holland, on the grounds of a *castle* one of his wealthy supporters had given him, and gave the most astounding speech to thousands of people who were expecting him to announce *his Coming as a….messiah.* He said *No, I'm not who you are expecting. I can only teach you one thing; and that is how to be totally and unconditionally free.*"

"Unbelievable." Harry gasped.

"Yes! So this young Indian boy started speaking about trying to live in the moment--fresh—without the baggage of our past conditioning, and that we didn't need to have organized religions to find God. He was so charismatic and his message so new that Annie simply said: *He has come.* "And yet he wouldn't be a Theosophist—he was the most anti-guru Guru they'd ever heard speak—and full of passion and conviction."

Harry nodded. I sensed right then that this was going to change something, but I didn't know what. Harry stared at me with his tired blue eyes. He was finishing a full day in the pottery shop and his pants were covered with clay dust. He probably was ready for us to make dinner.

I stroked the cover of the red book. I couldn't stay quiet: "...but you know what is really sad, is that she never knew that her adopted son, Krishnamurti, really did grow into being just what she had proclaimed him to be—one of the world's great spiritual leaders. The prediction became true."

"Oh I remember him now. He was very popular in the 1960's and '70's when everyone got on board with the idea that God was within us and we could follow our own path to God. We could create our own lives and reality. Right?"

"Exactly." Harry got it. I smiled back, glad that he remembered. "Honey, there's one other thing. I don't know why I have to do this, but I must…and then we'll make dinner." I paused.

"What?" He looked a little unnerved now.

"I have to find out what this means for me. There's something strange happening here—look! Our astrology charts are so similar—look—we were born 100 years and 5 minutes apart! I opened my notebook to our charts. I don't get this! And I don't understand about these 'invisible worlds' she talks about so much…." I paused, and Harry's face twitched. "And look at this—I pointed to a quote on a page I had ripped out of a journal I had kept years ago. It read: "*No soul that aspires can ever fail to rise; no heart that loves can ever be abandoned. Difficulties exist that in overcoming them we may grow strong, and only those who have suffered are able to save.*"

"You know who wrote that?" I asked. "Annie Besant. I just found it. I don't remember where or when I found it." I paused and looked out the window again, wondering how my ever-patient Harry would take to my next piece of news.

"Anyway, that's not important, what is important is that I've decided that I'm going to see this woman tomorrow. She's a psychic—a really respected one. She's supposed to be great." I paused. "And I'm going to pray for Annie to come through her to me, to see why I'm so drawn to her life. Then I'll know."

"Know what?" His lips tightened.

"I don't know." My head dropped as I touched my chest and inhaled. "I guess I want to know why she's come into my life like this, at this time, with these astrological synchronicities, and why I feel such a heart connection to her."

It was quiet for a moment. When I looked up I could have sworn that the light outside the window had darkened into a luminous yellow. It looked as if a storm was approaching and the wind was whipping up the undersides of the leaves on the trees by our house. A branch snapped a harsh whack against the house. "You know, Harry, this could change my life; our lives."

"Elizabeth, you're going to make some kind of life decision based on a psychic?!"

"I don't know. Maybe I'll just find out if synchronicities like these really matter. They could, couldn't they? I mean astrology is based on the synchronicity of your birth time and place—Carl Jung said our birth time was the most important synchronistic moment of our life."

Harry looked like he was going to launch into a crusade of reasonableness when I interrupted him.

"It's all 'flapdoodle' right?" I grinned and narrowed my eyes at him, knowing that that one word had more meaning than he'd ever guess. It was the favorite expression of Annie's Russian mentor, Madame Blavatsky, whenever she got annoyed.

"Elizabeth, I can accept the psychological astrology you practice...but psychics and all this Krishnamurti stuff; it's so....dense...so occult. It almost gives me the creeps, like this weather now."

I saw our dog dash inside for cover as the sky opened up and dropped its rain. My voice became a whisper: "Why hasn't anyone told her story from her point of view, Harry? Even this book has got an attitude. Why has she been overlooked in history—erased? Because people thought she was crazy? People criticize what they don't understand—but nobody knows this story; her story; the true story! Not the drivel the newspapers of her time wrote about—they just mocked her and the historians simply wrote her out of history. Now she's collecting dust on the shelves.

"So maybe you're the one to tell her story." Harry stated.

The next morning I went to see the psychic. And I prayed. I drove over to a wood-shingled colonial house in downtown Newport, parked my car and walked over to the address on my paper. I checked the number again: she was on the third floor. On every step of the way up I repeated Annie's name like a mantra as if to give me courage. I tried not to think of the fact that I didn't really like psychic mediums, that I was afraid of knowing too much, and that I'd never wanted to know more of the future than what an astrology chart could show me. Astrology honored free will, and the ability to change one's fate. I didn't know if most psychics have that point of view; but it was too late to think of that now. I knocked.

Candace was a little older than I expected, and she wore a long skirt, peasant blouse, with even longer earrings and graying ringlets framing a delicate face. She had a sincere smile that beamed at me, as she led me to a small round table on which was a lit candle, tarot cards, and assorted books. There was a faint herbal smell coming from the kitchen. "Would you like some tea?" she asked. I took her raspberry blended tea and sipped it with my skepticism growing at the same rate as my hope. I found it hard to drink the tea.

Candace looked down at my hands. "Do you wear that bracelet a lot?" she asked me. I nodded. "Could I hold it?" I handed it to her, and she closed her eyes. I waited for what seemed to be almost too long.

The first words out of her mouth were: "I hear the name Ann…Annie. She's saying something about the two of you collaborating on a project…?" She looked up at me. I stopped breathing and just nodded my head, yes. Another even longer pause. "Ah…does she live in New York City or somewhere close?" I shook my head no, but smiled. I had heard what I needed to hear in her first sentence. The rest was a blur. As I retraced my way downstairs I knew, with every ounce of my being, that I needed to write the story of Annie's life—and I needed to begin it now.

Two

Instant Therapy and a Treehouse to Dream In 1987

We were silent in the car on the way to the therapist's office. This was our third visit and the therapist ended our last session by saying she'd never met a couple in her office that got along as well as we did—she was baffled.

But today my face was still red from crying from the daily morning's phone conversation with mother—she wanted to come stay with us for the summer, which was fine, but she refused to accept that I needed "writing time" from eight to eleven every morning. Her unwillingness to accept any conditions around her visit made it into an either/or situation—I loved her or I didn't—she would come, with no restrictions, or she wouldn't come. I had to say no. Tears and pleading words ended every conversation with her.

What was even worse was the hollow feeling inside me when I looked over at Harry. He looked depressed, and I suspect I looked the same. There seemed to be nothing truly wrong with us, except that he was overstressed with working so much at the pottery shop, and I was overstressed trying to write a book as well as working at the pottery shop. Mothering our daughter Sarah was not hard; it had its sweet highs and tender lows, but mothering my mother was wearing me down.

Harry's face looked thinner and I hadn't seen the sparkle in his eyes in months. I noticed how cranky I was getting—the writing was going slowly and I didn't feel that deep connection to Annie I hoped for—and I didn't know all those little things writers need to know about their subject. How was I to find out? I was working alone in my room with a few books, my electric typewriter, and a shortage of new inspiration. I needed to be in California at the place where Annie had spent so much time, or in England where she had worked. I had yet to feel her "collaboration" with me on this project.

The hour was coming to an end. "So Harry," the therapist finally said, "what would you *most* like to do now? You're sounding like you need a break; something new…what would that be?"

"I don't know. I just want us to be happier." He squirmed in his chair.

Silence. She turned to me. "And what about you, Janet?"

I twisted my hands trying to find the words. "I want us both to be happier too. We're both feeling restless, irritable, and it's hard to say why. I'm nervous; scared. We're both in what astrologer's call the Uranus Opposition, and this passage calls for a big change in one's life…but we don't know what it is for us."

"And you're going through this too, Harry?" she asked. He nodded. She leaned over to him: "Tell me Harry, what would you like to do if you could do anything in the world—anything?" Harry pursed his lips, and then it looked like the proverbial light bulb went on in his head.

"Well if I had my druthers, I'd like to do what my father never had a chance to do. I'd like to go to California. Just drop everything, and go."

It was as if the earth shifted just then. I hadn't even told him that I'd been yearning to do some research on Annie at Krotona, the Theosophical Society, which was in Ojai, California. My eyes widened. "Let's do it Harry—let's just go! I mean it! You can make pottery out there as well as here! What do you think?"

We both laughed and nodded our heads. How can one's world change so fast? We left the office with our arms around each other and the hope for a new life.

We shocked ourselves with our gritty determination and sheer luck. We sold the house to the first person who saw it. And our shop? The manager of our pottery shop was thrilled to take over the shop as if it was her own. The "stars must have been aligned" with us.

I remember the moment when we told "the news" of our intention to move to our eight year old daughter, Sarah. It was like a photograph. She stood with one hand on the refrigerator door and was looking back at us...and instantly, one tear fell down her cheek. She was going to have to let go of all she was accustomed to; not easy for anyone, but then a huge smile broke through even stronger than the single tear. Perhaps she realized that we needed to do this as a family.

I also remember the moment when I told my mother we were moving. It too, was like a photograph: I was in bed early in the morning on the telephone, and mother told me that if I moved, she would commit suicide. Period. I tried pleading with her...I remember staring at a crack in the wall and wondering how this conversation would end. I kept explaining that we would stay in touch with visits and calls back and forth, and...that no matter what she decided to do or not do, that I loved her. And then, I hung up the phone.

And that's how we came to live in Ojai, California. We dropped everything and left—it took 6 months and 3000 miles to get to our new dream.

Luke, the realtor, was reluctant to show us the last house he had listed. This was the last day we had left to find a house before flying back to Rhode Island. Luke had showed us over-priced houses hanging precariously off cliffs in the high mountains of Santa Barbara and had shown us dark moldy homes under the oaks in Ojai. We were willing to take almost anything that didn't smell or look like the owner had just died or looked like it was the next statistic in an earthquake report. It shouldn't have been so hard.

It was the end of the day and the last listing he had. "This one is a bit of an embarrassment really, but I'll show you if you want..." I couldn't imagine any worse. It was the end of a week of looking at houses that were all wrong.

As we drove up the steep hill we passed a long row of cypress trees, till the road turned dry and dusty. We passed what looked like an abandoned sail boat hoisted on stilts on our left, and a long red barn on our right. There were a few palm trees and cactus. The view kept getting better and better.

"I hope they have the chickens out of the bathroom by now" Luke said. Harry and I looked at each other and burst out laughing. We weren't expecting a clean house after what we'd seen today, but "chickens?"

"Yeah, and there's probably a few people still living here." Luke said. "The house comes with…well let's see…. two trailers, a teepee, the boat you just saw, and a treehouse. Oh yeah… and more; it was a hippie commune." There was junk and stuff everywhere. But that's not what we saw.

The realtor curved the car around past the front of the long house and stopped at the edge of an orange grove that seemed to fall away for miles. We stepped out of the car and looked around….and around and around. There was an almost 360 degree view of mountains, sky, orange groves…and a gentle breeze that blew through some wind chimes. I heard the sound of a horse's whinny. And there in the distance I could see mountains with layers upon layers of thin clouds around them, looking like a Japanese painting.

My eyes teared up. Harry looked over at me—the two of us smiling like from ear to ear—and my tears began to fall. "This is it," I said, grabbing Harry and squeezing him so hard he laughed. "You don't even want to look inside?" he said, "To see the chickens in the bathroom?"

"It doesn't matter. Look at this!" I extended my arms like Eve showing Adam paradise. The view was breathtaking and the feeling was *freedom.*

Harry walked over to an orange tree and pulled an orange off. He held it in his hand and then smelled it. "I've never picked an orange from a tree!" he said. "But look at this—not too pretty." he said, his arms pointing to overhead electric lines crisscrossing the land like a spider's web.

"You could...bury them. Couldn't you, honey?" I believed he could do anything.

The realtor walked the land with us. "It's what's left of a hippie commune that actually closed up over a year ago. But I think there are a couple of people still here—illegally now. He pointed to the tree house, teepee and boat. But I'm sure they'll be gone soon."

"I want to be here, Janet—what do you say?" Harry was radiant. We hadn't even looked inside the house.

"Absolutely." I looked at the avocado and pomegranate trees and thought I'd gone to heaven.

"It's five acres and $250,000, as is…right?" Harry grinned. "We'll take it, Luke."

And that's how we got to live in the long narrow house with a treehouse, a barn for the pottery, an occasional horse that wandered through the backyard, and a nest of baby rattlesnakes in the front lawn. I planted jasmine and arranged to get our furniture moved, while Harry found contractors to bury the electric and some workers to take all the "extras" away—about 4 large dumpsters full.

The old hippies left and the "new hippies" moved in. But we certainly didn't need all that chicken wire, sheet metal and not even the cannabis growing in the backyard. Instead we had a hot tub installed, so at dusk we could stare at what the locals called the "pink moment" at the end of the day when the mountains would light up with a luminous shade of rose. And at night we'd look up to the sky to see more stars than we'd ever seen in our lives. At long last Sarah had a place to ride her bike, a warm "tub," and happy parents. And mother, well, she took up oil painting with a passion…and the phone calls less frequent.

Sarah and I also found a place we could dream in—we would hang out in the treehouse with a view that dropped away for miles and miles till the mountains rose up again. Sarah would bring her "pretty ponies" up there and I would bring my books. It was there that I read my first book by Krishnamurti. Never had I read anything so dense, but when I stopped to look out at the view, all the rationality dropped away, and I understood what he was talking about. I guess that's the only way to read a mystic. ~

Three

From Treehouse to the Great Hall and Back Again

"Never forget that life can only be nobly inspired and rightly lived if you take it bravely and gallantly, as a splendid adventure in which you are setting out into an unknown country, to meet many a joy, to find many a comrade, to win and lose many a battle."
— Annie Besant

The first month in Ojai I spent most of my free time in the treehouse alone. I would read and meditate and stare out at the mountains and ask myself: What would Annie have me do? But honestly, it was clear what she wanted, I was simply not doing it. I was procrastinating and scared.

I knew that Annie's spiritual center--the Theosophical Society--called Krotona, was less than a mile away—in fact, from the front yard I thought I could spot the faint image of orange tiled roofs over stately white stucco buildings. But instead of going there, I would retreat to the treehouse to read books. Annie, and all the people in her life were characters in my head: my private dream. Perhaps I was a little unwilling to share it.

What if I didn't like the people at Krotona or what if they didn't like me? I could be told I wasn't a card holding Theosophist and had no right to be "prying." Maybe they wouldn't say it like that, but still…I could be disappointed by who I found there: cold indifferent people, or worse yet, occultists with penetrating eyes who would find me unworthy of their secrets. What were those secrets anyway?

Why was I procrastinating? Did Annie ever procrastinate? I believe things happen at the time they're meant to happen, and I was a believer in that—all astrologers believe that to be true. So I wasn't going to push getting there, but rather wait for the right moment to go there.

In the meantime, back at the treehouse, I read everything I could find on occultism, Annie, and Krishamurti. Because Annie and Krishnamurti had once lived in Ojai, I was beginning to meet people who knew them, but it was still just a beginning. Right now, I was trying to understand why spiritualism and Theosophy was sweeping with such power through England and America at the turn of the century. Why would Americans and the upper class British, —such perfectly rational people— be swayed into believing that "Masters" existed on other planes of life and that they actually communicated with us? Why did anyone believe that?

Some writers said it was a backlash to the rational science and engineered industrialism that kept people in factories or in limited social roles. Or it might be that the Christian theology was being undermined by Darwinism.

It was easy to understand how the early Theosophists were like the old guard of the "New Age" with beliefs in reincarnation, karma and vegetarianism, and I liked that they upheld a public face that looked more like open-minded Unitarianism. However it didn't take much more reading to discover that there was an esoteric side to the group—a belief in spiritual Masters and invisible worlds—that wasn't shared openly with the average person... and that was me.

I knew that Krotona sat perched on 12 acres high on a hill, looking East over the Ojai Valley. Most people in Ojai had heard the names of Ojai's "Patron Sages" Annie Besant and Krishnamurti. They knew of Besant Road and many remembered the hundreds of people that used to arrive in town every spring to sit on their blankets on the lawns of the Oak Grove School to hear Annie's adopted son, Krishnamurti, speak. But not many people realized that these gatherings weren't just a phenomena of the

1960's but had their origin back in 1922 when Krishnamurti first came to the valley. He'd come in hopes that the hot dry weather in the valley would cure his sick brother of tuberculosis.

I was gathering facts. I found out that in the 1920's Ojai was the 'talk of the town' in nearby Hollywood, and people such as John Barrymore, Greta Garbo, Aldous Huxley, and many others made their way to Ojai to befriend the young and very handsome, Krishnamurti. Some producers wanted him to be the leading star in a movie on the Buddha, but it was Annie who had a bigger dream for Krishnamurti and Ojai.

Annie remembered that Helena Petrovna Blavatsky (or HPB as they liked to call her) had foreseen a new spiritual awakening happening in America, and Annie felt that it was in Ojai that this new spiritual center for the New Age would arise. (Her "New Age" was the astrological movement from the Piscean Age to the Aquarian Age...Yes, as the song says: "this is the dawning of the Age of Aquarius!") With that idea in mind very early in the century, Annie bought up hundreds of acres of land for several centers here—money she had made in her speaking tours across America—and put some of it into establishing a high school in the upper Ojai. She even bought the town newspaper.

In 1927, Annie spoke at the Ojai Valley Theatre, six years before her death:

> *"One of the beauty spots of the world is the Ojai Valley…mountains ring it round; it has remained secluded till recent times and is still but sparsely inhabited. The climate is superb; orange trees laden with golden fruit grow in parts of it, as well as apricots and lemons. The sun shines out from a sky of deepest blue, and as it sets behind the mountain peaks it paints the mountainside in various purples and violets. It paints a panorama that I have only seen rivaled in Egypt or in the rainy season in India. Such is the setting for the cradle of the new civilization in America."*

I began to know these things because we met our neighbor, Alisdair, the one with the wandering horse (and the one who released the chickens in the bathroom when our house was a commune.) It turns out that he was a wellspring of information about what to read, who to talk to, and the valley. He had been Krishnamurti's gardener in his later years, and from him I sadly discovered that "K" as he was known, had died just the year before we showed up in the valley.

Alisdair, the gardener who worked on Annie's land in the Upper Ojai, now worked for the famous potter and sculptor, Beatrice Wood. Beatrice was in her nineties at that time and she told him stories of how Annie had such a profound impact on her. Beatrice was surprised at how open and friendly Annie was to her when she was young and just a simple potter, and she mentioned that Annie was "open" but not naïve.

The day I made the decision to go to Krotona, I was the one feeling naïve and not so terribly open. I wore my favorite dress with the tapestry fabric across the top, and took a little more time with my make-up than usual, as I wanted to look older, wiser, and something more than what I was.

The first thing that caught my eye as I drove up the hill was the arched windows that looked over the beautifully kept rose gardens. I parked my car and took the path that led by the water fountain and around the building to the oversized front door. It was as beautiful as it was imposing.

Opening the wooden door, the air felt cool as my eyes adjusted to the dimness. A couple of antique chandeliers lit up the room and a white haired woman sat at a desk at the rear. I hoped she would stay there and let me linger awhile without having to talk right away. There appeared to be a library on my right and another room on my left.

And then I saw her—there was Annie! On the center wall of the main room was a huge portrait. She looked down at me as if she'd almost been expecting me. I knew her well; didn't I? I allowed the moment of meeting to settle into me.

The painting must have been done when she was about seventy years old, and the graceful lines of her long robes reflected her quiet dignity. But her face revealed much more. The corners of her mouth drooped slightly, perhaps revealing a sadness? But the eyes were clear, kind and steady, although the skin around her cheeks fell in weary folds. She sat proudly, her hand prominently placed on her knee—perhaps she wanted us to notice this unusual ring bequeathed to her by Madame Blavatsky. And I knew that beneath that hand was her wounded knee—a tell-tale mark left from leading the strike of the Match Girls.

I felt as if I had walked into my dream. All this time I had been privately obsessing and changing my life because of this woman who was up on *their* wall! Here she was real, not just a figment of my imagination. I felt a rush of excited energy come over me. And there, on another wall, was a smaller portrait of Krishnamurti.

I peered into the curved door leading to a library. No one was in that dark wood paneled library, a room that looked more like a backdrop for a scene in "My Fair Lady" than for a library in sunny California.

Slowly the white haired woman who'd been sitting in the back approached me. She stuck out her hands: "I'm Sylvia, so nice to meet you."

"Janet. Janet Spring." Sylvia's hands encircled mine as if we were old friends meeting again. "Ahh....this is a bit of a shock for me to be here." I looked up to the painting of Annie. "I've been writing about her—oh, not a lot or anything much, really, but she found me and... well...I'm here now, not in Rhode Island anymore. Hah! It's like in the Wizard of Oz, I'm not in Kansas anymore." A shiver ran through me. "It's like Annie was just a character in my head that nobody knew about, and now she's become real!"

Sylvia seemed to take on the look of the good Queen of the East. Or was it Glinda? She put her hand on my shoulder and led me to a large high ceiling room with a stage at one end. Could there be concealed paintings or statues behind those golden curtains? The room smelled of something—the place reeked of secrets.

"You must come to our meeting on Tuesday night in the Great Hall here. It's open to everyone." She led me to a window where I could see a pergola leading to a climbing water fountain and a grove of trees. "And walk around the gardens, visit the book store, wander through the community if you have time. Most of us who work here full time, live here as well." She stared at me for a split second longer than I was comfortable with, but seemed to catch herself: "The esoteric section is over there in that building, but they're closed this afternoon." Sylvia smiled at me as much with her eyes as with her lips. She paused, head tilted, and lowered her voice: "You have such a radiance about you, do you know that?"

I laughed. "I feel as if I'm in another world, a dream, and I love it." Then a deeper stirring rose in me: "Something in me has come home."

"I can tell. You were quite taken by that painting of Annie, weren't you?"

I nodded. She touched my hand. "I know this is sudden, but on Tuesday I was going to read this part of a speech Annie had once given....would you like to read it instead?" She took a piece of paper out of her pocket and held it out to me.

"These are Annie's words?" I said, taking the paper in my hands. I skimmed it, recognizing the words "I'd love to read this," I said.

~

On Tuesday Sylvia introduced me at the meeting after the preliminary meditation, piano music and the reading of notes about last Tuesday's gathering. There must have been about seventy-five people there; and I'd dare say no one was younger than me. Harry had accompanied me and sat smiling from the second row as I was called to the podium.

I rose to the stage feeling like an imposter and still wondering why Sylvia had given this to me so quickly. But then I had another impulse—to throw up. I remember that Annie once said that she often had the same impulse before a speech, and sometimes the more nervous she was, the better the talk. I dared to hope.

I took out the paper, fingers squeezing the sides of the podium. I looked out over the room of expectant faces and taking a large breath I began speaking the words Annie had written so many years ago in her autobiography.

At first my words were slow as I wondered if my voice would hold, and then I let go into all the passion and clarity that Annie was known for: I found another voice I barely recognized as my own. The words flowed easily as if I had written them:

> *"I have been told that I plunged headlong into Theosophy and let my enthusiasm carry me away. I think the charge is true—and let me say that more than all I hoped for in that first plunge has been realized. I know, by personal experiment, that the Soul exists and that my Soul, not my body, is myself; that it can leave the body at will; that it can, disembodied, reach and learn from living human teachers, and bring back and impress on the physical brain that which it has learned; and that this process of transferring consciousness from one range of being to another is a very slow process, during which the body and brain are gradually correlated with the subtler form which is essentially that of the Soul."*

I paused and looked up. Their eager eyes were on me, all except one. The room was absolutely silent; I felt upheld by their listening... except for one man. Someone had made room for a very old man to sit down next to Harry, and his head was drifting downwards onto Harry's shoulder. Oh dear...! I could see the head finally fell onto his shoulder but Harry's eyes remained fixed on me.

> *"This same path of knowledge that I am treading is open to all others who will pay the toll demanded at the gateway -and that toll is willingness to renounce everything for the sake of spiritual truth, and willingness to give all the truth that is won to the service of man, keeping back no shred for the self."*

When I stopped they stood up and applauded! I was stunned. As I descended to my seat I caught Sylvia's beloved smile. I stayed in a dream state till the meeting was over and a woman named Joy came over exclaiming: "Why it's almost as if Annie herself was delivering that speech!" I grinned. A small group of people stood around us as I introduced myself to each. It all felt so good and right. The feeling of being an imposter had gone. Like Annie, I too, plunged headlong into Theosophy.

How did I speak like that? I spoke it was if "I" wasn't there—only the message counted, the emotion, the reason to speak.

But one thing didn't feel right; it was my name. I didn't feel like Janet anymore, yet I wasn't Annie either.

Harry led me home congratulating me on my new speaking "voice." I could tell he was as surprised as I was. By morning I had found my new name. It had been brewing in my psyche for a very long time—as I'd never felt like a Janet and I had always felt very close to my mother's mother: Elizabeth. I would now be Elizabeth, and it even pleased Harry and Sarah. My mother was not pleased, but at least she didn't threaten suicide. In fact, she was doing pretty well, getting more involved in her oil painting, and doing some beautiful paintings of birds and nature in New England. Reinvention was not Annie Besant's territory alone; it was all of ours as well.

Two days later a reporter from the Ojai newspaper called. They had heard that I was writing on the life of Annie Besant and Krishnamurti. Could they do an interview with me? I was more than surprised and more than willing.

By the next week there was a photo of me in the local paper and an article in which I relayed the major events in Annie's life. As I held the newspaper I stared at the photograph. This woman looks like a serious writer, I thought. And her name was *Elizabeth Spring*.

I was in a stage of euphoria for that first day. But by the next day I noticed that it took longer for me to get to my desk—didn't I need new curtains in that room? By the third day I was complaining to Harry how hard it was to do this writing and didn't I need to upgrade that old electric typewriter to a word processor? The next day it was simply too beautiful a day to write inside...had I'd forgotten that almost every day in Ojai was sunny and warm?

Each morning there was a mountain of resistance that had to be shoveled aside before I sat down to write. Sometimes I thought how stupid I had been. Why didn't I just do this quietly and talk about it when it was done? Instead I had publicly committed to telling the story of Annie's life, and now all I could see were the hours in the day melding into one long and back-aching, eye-straining experience. And it was going to go on and on—my God, it could take a year...or more.

Harry reminded me how lucky I was to be able to use the library at Krotona while dreaming into the story back on our lovely little hilltop. I guess it was as close as one could get to a writer's paradise, but as all writers know, there must always be critics—and so I gave Harry my first ten pages to read. "What do you mean it doesn't quite work? It doesn't flow? You don't *feel* it! What's that supposed to mean?" I screamed at Harry as if he were an idiot. I waved my papers around. I cornered him as he tried to make an exit. "Don't just stand there and tell me it's not good—it has to be good!" I didn't open the door to my writing room for a week: I read, questioned, and despaired.

And then I went back. One day while I was *trying* to read Madame Blavatsky's great book: *The Secret Doctrine,* I saw Harry coming into the room. I slid the book to the side, trying to stuff it under a pile of papers as if it were pornographic. The book was too large; its frayed red and gold binding stuck out like loose hair.

"Hey, what's happening? Your eyes are at half-mast. You don't look happy, my dear, what's wrong?" He sat down beside me.

I needed to confess: I pulled out the heavy tome. "This is unreadable! Sentences roll on for paragraphs about avatars and planes of existence—no one could ever read this! And yet her life—oh, Harry, I think Blavatsky embellished her *genuine* psychic ability with these letters from the "Masters" that she created—letters that would mysteriously appear and even fall from the ceiling! She didn't need to do these tricks, these 'phenomena.'

"Sounds like Annie believed it though." Harry opened the book and read:

> *"The aim of this work is to show that nature is not a fortuitous concurrence of atoms, and to assign to man his rightful place in the scheme of the Universe; to rescue from degradation the archaic truths which are the basis of all religions; to uncover the fundamental unity from which they all spring, and finally to show that the occult side of nature has never been approached by the science of modern civilization."*

He snapped it shut. "Doesn't sound unreasonable; just wordy, kind of archaic. Why would Annie go for this?"

I stood up and started pacing back and forth: "I've been reading more about this—I think she was drawn to it because she had a basic religious nature and Theosophy declared that *all religions* are variations of an original world Wisdom, and it had a belief that there was a spiritual nature to *everything*...and that there was an evolution and perfectibility of man through its cosmology."

Harry shook his head and added: "Kind of like the *perennial philosophy*, Aldous Huxley wrote about; I read it years ago."

"Yes, and some of it makes sense in light of reincarnation: if true knowledge is a secret doctrine, then there must be a few wise ones who can pass it on...like the Rosicrucians who believe in a brotherhood of wise men. Many people believe that the Universe is full of evolving beings." I stopped and then it hit home. "And it dealt with Annie's *first and last grudge against God*—the problem of all the pain and the cruelty she saw--in this way she could see that *suffering was had a meaning, not random,* and part of a cycle of evolving lifetimes."

"You sound like you're on the council for her defense!"

"I am! I'm trying to understand. You know what I think?" My finger started wagging. "Her mother let her down, God let her down, and so did her husband, and Shaw---I think she turned to HPB as to a *mother*; a kind of melancholy mother that she could help. From everything I read, Annie comes across as a deeply loyal person, but this would mean that she'd turn a blind eye to faults once her loyalty was given." I stopped, sat down, and started jabbing my finger into the book.

I flipped through the pages and made my last case: "I like that Annie fought for the under-dog, I like that she was anti-racist, that she was a feminist—but this occultism—it's too wordy—weird!" My finger did a final jab.

"Now tell me what you really think." Harry laughed. "Don't get so upset. It's a good story and as they say, 'more may be revealed'—you don't have all the information in yet. So *for now* you know that Annie took the best of Theosophy and kind of cleaned it up; maybe a little white-washing in the books? Or perhaps, she just made it more readable—more understandable for the British."

I picked up the book reverently this time. "I suspect Madame Blavatsky had a hard life—people didn't understand her; they called her a 'priestess of the occult.' I read how she left Russia as a young girl and wandered around the world, dressed up like a boy, hanging around with swamis and yogis in Egypt and Tibet. That's how she learned some of this...." I stroked the cover.

"And you know what, Harry? I wonder if there were Masters living somewhere in Tibet, who had real powers to do all the magical things that Madame herself later did?" I waved my hand in the air accentuating a sleight of hand. "Who knows, maybe there are Masters on the 'Other Side' or people who can guide us? Maybe all the people we've loved and who have died are there on the other side, willing to help us..." *And Annie too, I thought.*

"How can anyone really know?" Harry stood up and started leaving my study, then turned back. "You've got quite a story there—and my guess is that you don't even know half of it." He looked at me and grinned from ear to ear as if he knew what that was; I surely didn't. Then I closed the door to my study and went back out to the treehouse.

But this time instead of reading, I closed my eyes, took some deep breaths and began meditating. Once my mind stopped jumping around, I sent out a couple of long soaring "Oms" across the valley and settled into a quiet receptive space… wondering if I could pierce the veil between the worlds.

Four

The Cure for Procrastination

"If a doctor had written me a prescription for a pill to treat my procrastination, I wouldn't have taken it…it's not so terrible. I believe in the divine timing of events."

The Krotona library was relatively small, although it had a balcony for rare and first editions that only the librarian could access. I had come here this morning simply to browse and to see if anything "jumped out at me."

I ran my fingers along one old bookcase, and stopped when I came across a book on the Swiss psychologist, Carl Jung. I knew that he was one of the first to write about synchronicity; the idea that there could be a connection between two events or two people that had no rational causal connection. I knew that most people dismiss it as chance or serendipity, but many consider it to be a phenomena wrapped in mystery.

As I perused the book I learned that synchronicity has sometimes been called a *collaboration with fate.* How interesting—was I simply "ripe" for a synchronistic moment to occur that day I found Annie?

I put the book down and gazed out the arched window. No books had popped out at me. I hoped I would ferret out what I didn't know of theosophy from these old books or the "old timers" at Krotona. In talking with the librarian it seemed to be accepted that most of the esoteric secrets were now an integral part of modern psychology and spirituality, and that wisdom was not concealed for just the few in an inner circle anymore. Ideas like the "theory of attraction" and "as it is above, so it is below" were familiar concepts, especially in astrology.

I took one more walk around the room and found an old slim book at random. It was published in the 1920's and I flipped through it till I landed on a page that had the word "Wedgwood." The writer was discussing a man named James Wedgwood, who was in the early esoteric circle of Theosophists. Wedgwood was from the family made famous for their pottery, but what I read was disturbing. It was alluding to the fact that he believed that "truth" was not of ultimate importance in occultism, and should give way to loyalty. If there was a choice between helping someone to whom one had a duty and protecting an organization, or telling the unvarnished "truth" one should defer to one's loyalty. This was seen as a form of camouflage as "ordinary people" would be quick to judge, and judge incorrectly—so that different standards of morality applied to occultists and to people who didn't have the training and sensibilities of those who had the ability to "see more."

That was a most unappealing quality, but not totally unfamiliar. The Tarot cards were also a way to convey esoteric wisdom and Truths, but in a hidden way that required study to understand the meaning. However, this esoteric elitism in Theosophy felt like a little red flag, and I resolved to remember the name, Wedgewood, in light of what I'd just learned.

Driving home, my mind minced over these ideas, reminding myself that delving for Truth wasn't terrible; the only terrible thing would be *to not* to take up the quest, no matter what I found. Truth came before loyalty for me. I loved Krotona but I still had to delve for all the facts. And, I told myself that procrastination was waiting for the right time; because in time, what was most true would emerge.

When I got home I walked into my study and sat at the desk. I didn't like that last piece of information I'd found and I didn't like sitting inside, looking out at yet another beautiful Ojai day. The writing had been going better, but I still hadn't felt Annie's presence in the writing process. Maybe I needed to get out for a while—

I jumped back into the car and headed down the hill wondering where to go. The last few days I distracted myself by doing every errand I needed to do…now what?

As I drove East, the morning sun was well up and over the Topa Topa mountains. Purple bougainvillea's climbed over the fences that lined the road, marking off the acres of orange groves. As I drove I remembered reading about Annie's experience when she drove down this very same road, and then went up the Dennison Grade to the "Upper Ojai" and to a special spot to look out over the Ojai Valley. Ah…that's where I would go!

Our new friend, Alisdair, the gardener had told me exactly where this spot was located underneath a particular tree. Why hadn't I been there yet?

The curving roads and heights were dizzying, yet the closer I got to my personal mecca the more excited I became—I was being drawn here for sure. Annie would finally come to me in some way! As I rounded the last curve, I saw the singular large Oak tree in a meadow of spring flowers—it stood there by itself, as if it had been waiting from 1927 till now—sixty years—for someone to notice more than its beauty.

I walked over to the tree, careful not to step into any gopher holes or worse. I laid my sweater on the ground and with a careful appraisal of the view, sat down cross-legged. I took a few deep breaths. I opened my eyes and drank in the gracious steep curves of the distant mountains and the sharp peaks of the nearby ones. No wonder they had made the old movie "Shangri-La" here—it looked more like the Himalayas than any American mountains I'd ever seen. The rows of orange trees looked like curving lines over rounded hills, and I could see the village of Ojai in the distance. Annie had purchased 700 acres of land here the first day she saw it; the soaring vista must have done it; she must have been hoping that this was the place where the "new consciousness" would arise—the dream of Madame Blavatsky.

I sat there awhile feasting on the view, and then drifted into meditation. I prayed to Annie to send me a sign; to let me know she was here, now. A gentle breeze moved through my hair. Two enormous condors glided on the currents as I watched their easeful movements with awe, as they danced with each other effortlessly. How beautiful these large winged birds were… but what was I to do here? Was I going to continue to "reach" for Annie? Yes; I asked for a sign that she was present.

I waited. I closed my eyes. There it was again—the thought that drained me of all energy. What if my procrastination was a shield against my fear of not being able to write this story? That's what scared me the most; that even though I believed I had been called to write Annie's story, maybe I wouldn't be able to reach into those interior places to draw out what needed to be expressed.

I opened my eyes and the mountains spoke to me of belief. Deep old grounded knowing—they were a living proof of the God of the Earth. As I looked around me, the line between sky and mountain trailed like a story, and it didn't falter or stop; it encircled me. Although I knew I could only see part of the full circle, I knew it was there, just like I could only see so much of God. I breathed in the mountains and they soothed me.

But then a knot began forming in my stomach. The line where mountain and sky met was not a complete circle around me after all; I'd have to go higher to get a 360 degree view. I'd need to find a place where there was no interference or resistance, but that's almost impossible. Is that what I needed to write this story? Perfect reassurance? Why couldn't I just have the faith that what I have is enough? Was I going to commit to this work or not?

I remembered that indecisiveness is descriptive of the astrological aspect of a person with their Sun sign conjunct Neptune, and I had that aspect; that particular astrological cross. However to reinvent yourself you must have faith in your Self and your decisions. How could I do it? I remembered that Annie loved ritual—maybe I could create a little ritual.

Spotting a few flat stones across the meadow I walked over and brought them back to my spot beneath the tree. Piling them on top of each other I created something between an altar and a small 'cairn' sculpture. I was pleased. On this altar I could hold my belief.

There was my altar; but what to put on it? Could I find something that was a part of me that could be added to this sacred mound? Was there something precious I could leave there? Something in my bag I always carried? I shuffled through it, but there was nothing. And then I remembered: I had worn my favorite earrings that morning. Touching my ear I released one large round earring and starred at it. Two long beaked birds with wings outspread came together touching a mandala circle in the center.

Yes, this was it! I put one single earring on the top of the flat stone and prayed to Annie with words of thanks. I remembered reading how she liked ritual, and here was my ever-so-humble ritual: a place, a symbolic token, a prayer…and something else; that little bit of "numinosity" I felt when I looked up to see two huge birds circling overhead. Being here on Annie's land reached across time, and the birds on the earring and the encircling birds in the sky were synchronistic. They resonated and echoed within. And so with wondrous eyes, I bowed to this sacred place and retreated back to the car, drove down the hill, and made my way across town to the other hill on the other side of the mountain.

When I returned home Harry was gone and though everything looked the same, I felt different. As I walked past the jasmine-covered pergola, a hummingbird quivered nearby. My watery eyes made it look even more luminous. It was getting close to noon; I had better get to my work. I grabbed a large glass of water and went to my writing room.

The silence was palpable. I looked at the word processor and then let my hands glide along my bookshelf. All my favorite books were there, as well as the English fern my mother gave me which I carried across the country. And there was the silver trophy I'd received in college for winning first place at the debating society. What a surprise that had been—I had given my first talk in speech class and the instructor asked if I would give that talk at the debating society that very afternoon. I spoke on my experience of helping a young woman I knew who was institutionalized in a state mental hospital. I pleaded for the necessity for everyone to do something; to not let these people languish in appalling conditions. I won first place.

I sat at my writing desk. Could I ever do anything meaningful like that again? Could I ever be a really good writer? Could I, in some small way change the world just a little, by telling Annie's story? I had to at least try.

Five

The Story Begins: Mothers, Husbands, and Other Impossibilities

"She tried to follow Truth." This was to be Annie's epitaph. It had been her request from an early age, and an odd one, considering that she humbly added tried to follow Truth." Could she have guessed that each chapter of her life would be a relentless pursuit of Truth, of self-reinvention, of swinging from martyrdom to leadership, from defeat to victory and then more..? Each one nobly trying to follow Truth…?

"You have always been too religious," Annie's mother complained.

"Yes," she agreed. "When I pray, I ask Him to kiss me with the kisses of His mouth; for His love is better than wine."

Her mother must have winced, yet this is what Annie wrote in her autobiography when she was forty-one years old.

Annie was a passionate Christian as a young woman and was never non-religious, even when she became an "avowed Atheist" in her thirties. She once confessed to George Bernard Shaw: "If religion be morality touched by emotion, then I was the most religious of Atheists." Shaw never liked her earnestness, a trait he found most unappealing in any woman. But it was true, in Annie's movement from one crusading 'religion' to another there was a consistency: all her faiths were linked by a personal crusade for social betterment and the deep desire to find meaning behind the suffering she saw around her.

Annie Wood Besant had a difficult start in life. She was born in England in 1847, a female at a time and place which valued male children. Her father died when she was very young, leaving her mother to pour her time, energy and money into educating her son, as was done at the time. Annie competed for her mother's attention and wanted to be educated to be as smart as her brother, so she read voraciously and beyond her years, intent on proving her worthiness.

But Mrs. Wood had other ideas for her daughter, and at the age of eight Annie was sent away from home to be educated by an evangelical tutor, Miss Marryat, while her brother stayed at home with her beloved mother and went to Harrow, the nearby private school. Annie had an excellent education with Miss Marryat, yet being so devoted to her mother, she suffered from deep loneliness. Her unrequited love of her mother became as great as her desire for Christ, and both were to let her down at her times of greatest need. This was, perhaps, her first defeat.

After a proper Victorian education, Annie was led into a hasty engagement at the age of 18 to an austere minister, the Reverend Frank Besant. He would be a poor substitute for Christ; a matter-of-fact man who enjoyed mathematics more than theology, a man could never live up to the yearnings of Annie's heart. He was a serious, unambitious man with conventional expectations.

Shortly after their engagement was announced, Annie recognized her mistake, and *pleaded* with her mother to end what would turn into a disastrous marriage. Her mother, having once announced the engagement, refused the embarrassment of repealing it. She would not allow it.

Typical of many of the young women of her time, Annie had been taught nothing of sexuality or that she would lose what few legal rights she had by being married. Annie liked to write short stories as a young woman, and little did she know that every penny she earned by selling her stories would now belong to her husband, Frank. He also preferred that she not write under her own name.

Despite all her instincts, and with the pressure of her mother, she convinced herself that being a minister's wife would bring opportunities for heroic acts of self-sacrifice—she could tend to the sick, bring them food, and care for their souls. And so she married.

Annie's first child was a boy, Digby, and eighteen months later, her second child, Mabel was born. Mabel was a sickly baby and fell desperately ill of whooping-cough. For weeks she lay in hourly peril of death.

As Annie says in her autobiography: "*We arranged a screen round the fire like a tent, and kept it full of steam to ease the panting breath; and there I sat, day and night, all through those weary weeks, the tortured baby on my knees. I fought with Death for my child. At length, one morning the doctor said she could not last through the day, and took a bottle of chloroform and put a drop of it on a handkerchief till the drug soothed the convulsive struggle.*"

Mabel's life was saved, but this was the beginning of the end of Annie's faith. If God was all good and all loving, how could he allow such suffering, such evil?

It was just after this time that she resumed her studies of the Bible, determined still to be a good minister's wife, but much to her dismay she discovered that the four synoptic gospels in the Bible didn't align themselves as one story—she lined them up in columns and saw that their reports of Jesus's life didn't match.

Talking with other ministers didn't help; she was advised to pray more and read less.

The marriage slid from bad to worse. Frank had recently become the pastor of a poor rural church in Sibsey, Lincolnshire, England, and was struggling to keep up appearances. His wife's passionate concern over religious dogma was embarrassing and incomprehensible to him. It was her business to think of the comfort of the family, and leave the theology to him.

Annie endured listening to Frank's sermons on the glory of God's grandeur and grace, while she threw herself into parish work. Maybe by helping the poverty-stricken families in their farming district she could find her sense of mission. What she found instead was great poverty aggravated by continuous child-bearing and alcoholism.

In her book, *Autobiographical Sketches*, Annie remembered one case where the husband was out of work and 'had taken to drink.' She found his wife in their one room cottage lying in bed, with a sick child on one side of her, and a dead baby on the other side. The smell inside the cottage was something that Annie never forgot; it pierced through any illusions she had struggled to maintain.

The meaning of human suffering and the nature of a benevolent God could be debated, despaired over, or cosmically understood, but one thing would always be the first thrust of Annie's pen: the absolute necessity of ameliorating intolerable social conditions and ignorance.

It was at this time that Annie discovered a new idea for service—a way which would give people control over their lives and change the conditions of poverty. She came across an obscure pamphlet on birth control, and realized if the women in the village knew about this there would be fewer deaths and less hungry mouths to feed. She pleaded with Frank to allow her to share it, but he came to an astounding conclusion—what Annie needed was to have another baby herself, not to be running all over the village spreading strange ideas. Discussion finished. Annie hid the little book and secretly vowed that someday she would do something with it.

It was all getting to be too much for her: *"Because I had not yet learned to live for hope for man, and had lost my hope in God,"* she wrote in her autobiography, *"I began to feel that I could endure it no longer."* Frank was not only impatient with her, but at times, violent. Annie considered suicide--the bottle of chloroform was still in the cabinet. As she wrote:

> *"I uncorked the bottle and was raising it to my lips when, as though the words were spoken softly and clearly, I heard: 'O coward, coward, who used to dream of martyrdom and cannot bear a few short years of pain! A rush of shame swept over me, and I flung the bottle away...."*

Instead she retaliated against Frank by refusing to receive Holy Communion in church on Sundays. Annie declared she would not live a lie and act on what she did not believe.

Meanwhile her mother lay dying. It was a good excuse to get away from Frank for a while and to live with her mother. But mother was heart-broken at Annie's renunciation of Christianity. She had always declared that Annie's greatest fault was that she was 'too religious" but now this new stance was too much.

Disregarding Annie's attempts to explain her position, Mrs. Wood put Annie to the test. It became Mrs. Wood's dying wish that Annie receive Communion with her, because she said, "I would rather die and be in hell with Annie than saved without her." Surely Annie must love her mother enough to do this.

The melodrama that ensued must have been high drama from the accounts of the tears and anguish recorded in Annie's autobiography. Her desire to please and appease her mother, combined with her insistence to Frank that she could not live a lie, put her in quite a squeeze.

But Annie was very resourceful and managed to pull off quite a coup. After seeing innumerable ministers who flatly refused to get involved, Annie found one who agreed to administer Communion to both of them, despite the fact that Annie didn't consider herself a Christian in the strict sense of the word. Seeing Annie's pain and love for her mother, the liberal minister declared it "folly to make words into dividing walls between earnest souls who were trying to follow moral laws…."

So the deed was done, and Mrs. Wood died in peace, and Annie, not being a believer anymore, suffered no guilt. Annie had just pulled off the first of her attempts to reconcile the irreconcilable.

Annie had nothing uniquely her own. She had not come into herself yet. In her *Autobiographical Sketches,* she noted that her voice was the first to come—and quite unexpectedly. It happened one afternoon in early spring. She had been feeling restless and distraught, and so decided to lock herself in her husband's old stone church and play the organ. Usually this helped, but today it wasn't enough.

Looking up at the pulpit she felt a twinge of regret—oh, if only she had been born a man with religious passion, what sermons she'd preach!

Impulsively she sprang up the steps of the wooden pulpit and looked out the through the shaft of dusty sunlight that cut across the aisle and began to speak. Her rich voice swelled and echoed down the aisles and under the stone arches, filling her with awe.

She barely recognized her own voice. All her pent up passion broke into balanced sentences—she spoke about the sources of inspiration; her voice resonating musically as she appealed to the hearts and souls of her imaginary listeners. At that moment she knew the gift of speech was hers.

At a later date she wrote about inspiration in a pamphlet called "Avataras" and it might have been quite similar to her private sermon that day:

> *"Have you ever been drawn away for a moment into a higher more peaceful realm when you have come across something of beauty or art? Have you for a time lost sight of the pettiness of earth, of trivial troubles, and felt yourself lifted in a calmer region, beyond the light of common Earth? Have you ever stood before some wondrous picture where the painter has lit the canvas with all the hues of beauteous*

color? Or have you listened while the divine spell of music has lifted you...Ah, if you have known any of these in life's desert, then you know how all-prevading is inspiration..."

And that's the way Annie was always to speak: with no notes, no gestures, no strutting on the stage. Annie's would continue to speak all her life: at Queen's Hall in London she gave one of her first talks on the "Political Status of Women" and in 1911 she spoke at Albert Hall to an audience of 10,000 as part of a demonstration on woman's suffrage. She was a born orator. Some of her language sounds old-fashioned now, but she instinctively knew how to touch the heart and wrestle with the intellect.

At barely five foot two inches tall and with no microphone, how did she project such courage and deep belief? In her old age Annie was once to remark whimsically that she ought to be a good orator because she had been practicing for innumerable lifetimes; particularly in an incarnation as the martyred monk, Bruno, and the woman philosopher, Hypatia. It seems to be the same question as to ask where did

Mozart get his genius at such an early age? This is another case in which the theory of past lives seems a plausible explanation.

But now—here was a first taste of this gift—and spell-bound by the sense of her voice and half-dazed—Annie walked down the narrow steps, out of the church, and out of the life of Frank Besant forever. She had found her voice. It was 1873 and Annie was 26 years old.

Six

Speaking For Herself

After leaving Frank, Annie survived by writing a series of pamphlets which attacked church dogma; tracts with names like "On Eternal Torture" and "Natural Religion vs. Revealed Religion." She had taken Mabel with her, but had reluctantly agreed to leave Digby with his father. Life wasn't easy, but it was better than living with Frank. Later in life Annie wrote:

"No soul that aspires can ever fail to rise; no heart that loves can ever be abandoned. Difficulties exist only that in overcoming them

we may grow strong; for they who have suffered are truly able to save."

What a comfort it could have been to her to hear those words spoken then! But at the time, the only comfort she felt came from a sixteen page weekly newspaper called *The National Reformer.* The paper was the mouthpiece for a group called the *National Secular Society*, an organization devoted to the ideas of the new Freethought movement. Although it was anti-church and proclaimed atheism, it was actually much like a religion with its Sunday meetings, its lecture halls and sermons. There was even a Secular Hymn Book.

Stimulated by what she'd heard about this group and its elevated idealism, Annie went to hear the head of the Society, Charles Bradlaugh, speak on a spring evening in the summer of 1874. She was moved by his words and his presence. He believed what she believed, and she felt an instant kinship. He must have felt the same, for straight away he offered her a job as a columnist and reviewer at his newspaper, *The National Reformer.*

Charles Bradlaugh was forty years old at this time and was a self-made man. His mother had been a nursemaid and his father a simple clerk. His formal schooling ended at the age of eleven, but he immediately took a job as a law clerk and began his self-education. His studies in law resulted in his becoming one of the most feared advocates for the "people's causes" in the English courts. He had married an artisan's daughter, had two children by her, and by the time he met Annie, his wife was hospitalized with alcoholism and Bradlaugh was struggling to pay for his daughters' education in boarding school. Here's how Annie describes him when she first heard him speak:

> *"He was a large man with a grave, quiet, stern, strong face, a massive head, keen eyes...his voice grew in force ad resonance as he went from point to point in his speeches, till it rang out like a trumpet. Was this the man I had heard the newspapers describe as a blatant agitator, an ignorant demagogue?"*

Charles quickly became Annie's mentor and inspiration—he taught her the art of public speaking. She already had the gift, and she only needed to learn the fine points of reasoning and elocution.

She was fond of quoting one of his lessons: *"You should never say you have an opinion on a subject until you have tried to study the strongest things said against the view to which you are inclined."*

Annie's heart went out to him when she saw his living arrangements, and saw the extent he gave up all personal comforts for his duties to his family and his liberal cause. When his household had to be broken up to send his wife and children away, he sold everything to help support them, and took with him only a few things: his books, a tiny bed, a washstand, a chest of drawers, a table, a couple of chairs and one painting. He moved into two cramped rooms in which there was barely enough room for a man his large size to move in. His one attachment was to the painting, which he declared was "beyond all price." It was a dark oil painting, depicting a tired hurdy-gurdy boy sleeping in a doorway, with a monkey watching over its little master. The painting hung over the head of his bed on the only wall space unoccupied by his books.

It wasn't long before Annie began her career as a speaker with him. Together they traveled from one end of England to the other, speaking out on all sorts of liberal causes.

Annie's first speech was on the Political Status of Women and was well received, however in her later life she recalled: *"Before a lecture I am so horribly nervous, wishing myself at the ends of the earth, heart beating violently, and sometimes overcome by sickness. I cannot conquer the physical terror and trembling. People often say to me: 'You look too ill to go on the platform' And I smile feebly and say I am all right, and I often fancy that the more miserably nervous I am in the ante-room, the better I speak when once on the platform."*

That first winter before her lecture income was substantial, she travelled third class: in those times that meant sitting on hard wooden benches, chilled to the bone, with long waits for trains in the middle of the night. She slept in miner's cottages and shared their food and conversations on politics, God, and money.

She was now twenty-seven years old, very pretty and delicate, and made quite a curious impression wherever she went. She often dressed in dark silk dresses pulled in tightly at the waist, and cut down at the neck in a deep V, edged with white lace. Needless to say, the contrast between her looks, speech and her life of poverty drew attention.

While on their lecture tours, Bradlaugh and Annie were very conscious of conducting their lives with great propriety, but people still talked, and even the people within the Secular Society didn't like Annie's quick rise to power, for she was appointed vice-president of the Society in 1875. The "talk" didn't seem to bother Annie though, for as she wrote:

> *"I found myself in opposition to the Government of the day. I was against our aggressive and oppressive policy in Ireland, and India. I lifted up my voice in all our great towns, trying to touch the consciences of the people...against war, against capital punishment, against flogging, demanding national education instead of big guns, public libraries*

instead of warships—no wonder I was denounced as an agitator; a firebrand, and that all orthodox society turned up its respectable nose at me."

In 1877 Annie engaged in the first of her major battles, and although some people see the result of it as being the greatest achievement of her life, it also cost her the most. This new adventure was her first crusade dictated completely by her own free will. It was in defense of that pamphlet on birth control, and in the end, it cost her the custody of her daughter—an event she said, which almost killed her.

The Knowlton pamphlet was over forty years old at the time Annie discovered it, and its style was as antiquated and obscure as its title.

It didn't take Annie long to convince Bradlaugh of the necessity for them to go into partnership as publishers of this book, even with the full knowledge that their arrest for publishing an 'obscene pamphlet' was imminent. And indeed, within twenty minutes of the arrival of the pamphlet they had sold over 500 copies, and were sitting behind bars.

It was all good publicity and by the time they were released from their bitter sweet experience in jail, Annie had persuaded Bradlaugh that she would plead her own defense in the trial. And so she did…for two days Annie talked. Over 40,000 words were recorded as Annie went on about the appalling conditions of which she had seen so much: the mothers worn out by too frequent child bearing and the fathers despair because of their long working hours, lack of money and food.

As she said: *"I speak for the fathers who see their wage ever reducing and prices rising, for the mothers worn out with child-bearing, with two or three little ones around too young to guard themselves.… Gentlemen, do you know the fate of so many of these children?—the little ones half-starved because there is food enough for two but not enough for twelve? Gentlemen, your happier circumstances have raised you above this suffering."* She knew when to pause. *"Without the minimal comforts of life, one's dignity becomes degraded."* The courtroom would often burst into applause as she spoke.

The prosecutors' case was strong and simple. Anything that would give sexual information that explicitly was regarded as an attempt to deprave public morals.

The judge and jury declared the book obscene, but they also wanted to free Annie from any corrupt motives in publishing it. Obviously this lovely well-spoken lady had no lewd intentions. The twelve men on the jury were obviously in a state of emotional conflict; charmed and stirred to chivalrous yearnings by this oh-so-earnest young lady, and yet…that pamphlet was obviously obscene. The guilty verdict had to pass for the moment. But just as she was leaving the courtroom, the judge gave her another option: if she would agree to at least temporarily not sell the book she would not be sent to jail now—if she'd agree to pay a fine of 100 pounds. This she accepted. Annie had other plans.

As soon as she recovered from the ordeal of the trial, Annie set out to write and publish her own book on birth control. One that was modern, accurate, and clear in its intentions. With her elevated style it could not be considered obscene though it got the message across. Within two years the little book sold over a hundred thousand copies and within the next fifteen years, 500,000 copies were sold. Annie received a deluge of letters from grateful women all over the world.

Annie was the first woman in history to publicly endorse the use of contraceptives. In establishing the right to circulate birth control information, Annie had won her greatest battle in terms of relieving the agony and needless deaths and misery of young mothers. Everyone agreed that Annie had indeed won a heart-felt victory. That is, except for Frank Besant.

Frank had been following the trial with great interest. It was revolting to him to have his name—her name—associated with atheism and the notorious Bradlaugh. But the controversy over an obscene sexual issue was even worse. He decided he was going to get Mabel back. If his wife had gone to jail that would have been easy, but such was not the case. He was going to have to fight for Mabel in court.

It looked like he would have an easy time of it. Frank sued to deprive his wife of the custody of Mabel on the grounds of her Atheism and her association with Bradlaugh in publishing an indecent and obscene pamphlet. The click and clatter of tongues was loud and furious, and it seemed as if all of England was lining up to take sides. Newspaper scandals of those days were the prime topics of conversations, and even the aristocracy stooped to mudslinging.

A conservative member of Parliament mocked Annie and Bradlaugh by saying that he assumed that the birth control books had been published as the fruit of Bradlaugh's relationship with the godless Mrs. Besant. Everyone wanted to know the nature of their relationship. They were shadowed by detectives and journalists constantly, yet no impropriety could ever be found.

Annie was called to trial, and the judge, Sir George Jessel, was disgusted from the start with the idea of a woman defending herself in a court of law without recourse of a proper (male) lawyer. He was not impartial; he let it be known that he disapproved of the fact that

Annie had deprived Mabel of good Christian religious instruction. The irony of this did not escape the press, which flaunted the fact that a Jewish judge was prejudiced from the start because Annie did not believe in a Christian God.

Frank raised money for his trial from his vicarage, and Annie raised money from the working classes who made up her audience in writing for the *National Reformer.* Annie's arguments were not so eloquent in this trial; and now with her back to the wall she admitted that her husband had repeatedly struck and threatened her. She mentioned six occasions, and that he kept a loaded gun in his study and threatened to shoot her.

Frank denied every one of the charges and said they were imaginary and "the violence… if any, was done in the heat of the moment." Guns were allowed in homes, and domestic violence was as rampant as alcoholism then. These were not crimes.

Annie wanted to keep this trial closely entwined with the first trial, trying to make her personal troubles into universal issues, but the final judgment came down from the Judge himself, because of her lack of belief in a Christian God. Without this, she could never raise a child properly; she was declared an "unfit mother." This was the last time in history that the government was allowed to take a child from a parent because of "religious heresy."

In all of Annie's autobiography her only words of bitterness were against the judge who deprived her of her children. Yet she knew she had forced this situation against the warning of all her friends, and with the knowledge of the laws of 1879. Perhaps the success of the first trial gave her false courage.

Annie always referred to the loss of her daughter as the most agonizing experience in her life. By way of compensation she devoted herself increasingly to the suffering of women, children and the poor. Now haunted by the sense of the motherhood she had lost, she tried instead, to be a mother to all.

Seven

Of Match Girls, George Bernard Shaw, and Eleanor Marx

At this point in her life, Annie could have succumbed to one of those mysterious illnesses which confined nineteenth-century ladies to sofas and darkened rooms. The loss of her children would have broken the spirit of many women.

With the birth control pamphlets Annie had made a permanent contribution to the progress of women. But she also began to feel a growing sense of dissatisfaction and an inner emptiness that both scared and depressed her. But it was then that she found the drug of her choice—something that for the rest of her life she could not do without: *work.*

In the beginning, Annie survived by taking the money from her lectures and writing and plunging herself into studying science at the University. She studied botany and physics, as well as earning certificates to teach classes in these subjects. She said at that time: *"Let me say to anyone in mental trouble, that they might find an immense relief in taking up some intellectual recreation of this kind."* Without a family and children, and no direction, working and learning seemed reasonable.

Annie came out of the ordeal of the trials at first feeling closer to Charles Bradlaugh. Annie once admitted that she loved Bradlaugh more than any other man in her life. She deeply admired him, he touched her heart, and he had been such an inspiration—but that was not to last—Charles allowed his political life to take precedence over everything.

And they were moving in different directions; Annie's struggle for the poor was leading her into Socialism, whereas Bradlaugh had a fierce individualism that didn't mix well with that group. The feeling of loss was mutual, yet Annie felt that his "secularism" seemed to go only so far, and then stop. She was beginning to see it as being only so much rhetoric. Parliament appealed to Bradlaugh, but Annie thought it was too slow. She wanted action and as she said: *Who was really doing anything for the poor and the oppressed anyway?*

Her answer came in the person of Eleanor Marx, Karl Marx's daughter, a woman who was equal to Annie in intellect and out-spokenness, and who had an almost proprietary interest in Socialism. She denounced the Secularists as being bourgeois intellectuals, and claimed it was the Socialists who were actually throwing the potatoes into the plates of the poor. Or at least they were trying to...

Annie was intrigued. Eleanor was a hard-drinking, cigarette-smoking, raven-haired beauty, who also irritated Annie beyond all reason. First she had a way with men, and then the scathing attacks she wrote on Secularism in the newspapers rattled Annie's reasoning.

The problem was that the Socialists were calling attention to the real social issues of the day: the inadequacy of the school system, the problems of child labor, and the conditions of the factories. Annie had been trying to deal with these issues through charity work, benevolent leagues, and lectures. But it wasn't enough. She wanted to get out there and do something.

Inwardly she was in constant turmoil—and then the infamous straw that broke the camel's back appeared. For months the Socialists had campaigned for free lunches for the London public schools, arguing that it made no sense to buy books and pay teachers when the children couldn't concentrate because of hunger. London at this time was in the midst of a severe economic depression, and a large majority of families ate only one decent meal a day; in the evening. The children were being sent to school on empty stomachs. Aggravating the situation even more was that it was a cold, frigid winter—the poor were having a real battle just trying to keep warm.

Annie weighed the issues closely for weeks. Bradlaugh's staunch brand of individualism, in which the workingman pulled himself up by his bootstraps, had no room for "welfare" lunches. He wanted to convince government that they needed to provide jobs, not hand-outs. She knew she had to stand against Bradlaugh on this one; so in her Christmas column in the *National Reformer* she came out in favor of free lunches and she was fiercely pounced upon for her Socialist sentimentalism. She had taken the first step towards a new cause, a new life.

It was a slow and sad parting of ways between Annie and Charles, with his eye on Parliament, and Annie wanting to dig her feet in the trenches. Annie was not having an easy time making the transition from Secularism to Socialism, and even that wasn't a great fit. She was frequently ill with congestion of the lungs and having fits of losing her voice altogether. Bradlaugh was of no help to talk to, for he found the Socialists to be: *"a few poets, a few idiots and some others of whom I could not use such kindly words."*

Annie managed to get herself elected to the London School board and was starting to make some changes for the poor there, despite the fact that she was fighting off a depression. She could have continued to rise in political power while on the London School board—she was the first woman in British history to get elected to public office by being on the school board—and she had the connection with Charles in Parliament if she wanted to go in that direction. But it was not power Annie wanted—as she wrote:

> *"I finally convinced myself that there was some hidden thing, some hidden power, and resolved to seek until I found it, and by the early spring of 1889 I had grown desperately determined to find what I sought. At last, sitting alone in deep thought as I had become accustomed to do after the sun had set, filled with an intense but nearly hopeless longing to solve the riddle of life and mind, I heard a Voice that was later to become to me the holiest sound on earth, bidding me to take courage for the light was near."*

Annie did not know who or what that "Voice" might be at this time, but astrologically this was the time of Annie beginning to enter her "*Uranus opposition*" a time that brings radical change into our lives—a life passage that happens to everyone between the ages of thirty nine and forty-two. It often starts with depression and restlessness that leads to change, rebirth and renewal. Annie was reinventing herself yet again—an excellent choice for anyone at their Uranus Opposition. And she was writing her autobiography.

It took all the Irish charm and keen mind of George Bernard Shaw to outwit and win over Annie from her growing and uneasy depression. As Annie writes:

> *"At this time I met George Bernard Shaw, one of the most brilliant of Socialist writers, and most provoking of men; a man with a perfect genius for aggravating the enthusiastically earnest, and with a passion for representing himself as a scoundrel. On my first experience of him on the platform*

at South Place he described himself as a 'loafer' and I gave an angry snarl at him in the National Reformer, for a loafer was my detestation, and behold! I found that he was a writer with principles, and preferred starving his body to starving his conscience; that he gave time and earnest work to the spreading of Socialism, spending night after night in workmen's clubs; and that a 'loafer' was only his amiable way of describing himself."

Shaw made an interesting comment about Annie at this time: *"I attracted and amused Mrs. Besant for a time; but in the end the apparently heartless levity with which I spoke, made it very hard for her to work with me. She therefore became a sort of expeditionary force, always to the front when there was trouble and danger, leaving the routine to the rest of us, and taking the fighting on herself.* An *attempt to keep pace with her on the part of a mere man generally wrecked the man."*

What many don't know is that Shaw was very poor at this time, and Annie supplemented his meager income out of her own pocket by paying him to write articles for a new little magazine she created called *Our Corner.*

Between 1885 and 1887 Annie and Shaw were very close. How close they were is debatable; some people believe they were lovers, others do not. We do know that besides their love of debate, they spent many hours playing piano duets as well—Shaw had an easy mastery over the music whereas Annie struggled to keep up with him on the piano, and felt uneasy in the parlor parties he loved to attend.

She must have had high expectations of him which he didn't chose to live up to—in many ways they were not compatible spirits and it is a mystery why she loved this man who enjoyed lazily deriding almost everything Annie did. He had a definite distaste for commitment, and as he said to her: "*When the Revolution comes, you'll find me under the bed,*" and it seemed to be true in the affairs of the heart as well.

They must have been quite an odd pair, Shaw with his red hair and pointed sandy beard, mocking eyes, and snappy humor. And Annie; impulsive, intense, half puzzled, half annoyed by his refusal to be serious. At this time she had abandoned her Victorian clothes and dressed the part of 'the worker.' She often wore heavy lace-up boots, a short skirt, and a red scarf. Her short curly hair gave her a look of boyishness and her straightforward expressiveness gave her a provocative air.

This provocative air of hers made for lively meetings of the Fabians, as her Socialist group was called. These meetings were sometimes held at Annie's house on Avenue Road, with much "sherry and brandy inspired" discussions which often ended with Shaw and Annie playing piano together. However although Annie loved Shaw and loved many of the ideals of the Socialists, she didn't see herself as being an intellectual gentlewoman or a political dilettante, nor did she see herself as being a woman like Eleanor Marx.

Eleanor was a 'femme fatale', a woman who inspired jealousy in women and lust in men. She had an almost proprietary interest in socialism because of her father, Karl, and although active in the Society when Annie was involved, she later became a romantic tragedy—she committed suicide over the love of a science professor.

But it's true that Annie and Shaw loved each other, and the story goes that he asked her to marry him, but since Frank Besant wouldn't give her a divorce, she drew up a marriage 'contract' instead. The commitment unnerved him, and he withdrew. However Shaw was always fascinated by Annie, wrote about her in some of his plays, such as *Arms and the Man* and summed up his feelings for her by saying: *"Love me lightly love me long. That is how I loved and will always love, Annie Besant."*

Neither Bradlaugh nor Shaw accompanied Annie into her next public battle. Both men broke her heart; both men were emotionally detached and Annie wouldn't settle for circling the orbits of either of them. She was committed to following Truth, and what broke her heart the most at this time was the plight of the match girls of London. The girls working in the match factories were the most down-trodden oppressed group of workers in London and they were not protected by the

British Trades Union, which confined its activities to the organizing of *men only.*

This crusade, which caught Annie's attention, was the strike of the Match-girls in 1888 when Annie was forty-one years old. It began with William Stead, a pioneer of modern journalism, asking Annie's help in starting a "Law and Liberty League" which would defend all workers. Stead was the editor of a large newspaper, the *Pall Mall Gazette* and Annie was more than eager to help him in this, and she suggested that they also start a weekly paper to be the mouthpiece for this organization. Stead and Annie were of similar minds and temperament and they soon had a smaller newspaper, *The Link,* off the press, and out on the streets. The paper was sub-titled*: "A Journal for the Servants of Man."*

One of the first articles Annie wrote for this paper was titled, "White Slavery in London," and was the result of her investigation into the working conditions at Bryant and May's match factory. Annie had heard of the deplorable working conditions at the factory and so discreetly questioned a few unsuspecting girls.

She discovered that not only were the girls being paid the lowest wages of any working group in London, but they were being poisoned as well—their hair and teeth were falling out because of the constant inhaling of toxic chemicals.

In her most eloquent style Annie shocked all of London with the intensity of the misery she discovered. She then cleverly appealed to the shareholders of the company, pretending to assume that they were unaware of the problem: *"Did they know that these girls worked fourteen hours a day for wages of four shillings ten pence a week? While the stockholders dividends were increasing?"*

The expose aroused the anger and sympathy of everyone and the feeble excuses from the factory management were impotent. They tried to fire the girls who had talked, and in protest, a small band of girls gathered together and marched across town to Annie's office to beg for her help.

Annie organized the girls into a sustaining strike that lasted three weeks, and called them together in weekly meetings where she inspired and encouraged them to hold out and not return to work. She moved among them like a fairy god-mother and put into each girls hand the money necessary for her to live on for that week.

During their weeks with no pay Annie had to raise money from other individuals to carry them over; even Shaw himself threw in money that he had scraped together from the pockets of his friends. The factory finally declared defeat. The strike was an enormous success because not only were the working conditions improved, the pay raised, and hours lowered, but the factory became exemplified as a model factory for others to emulate.

Annie had given the girls just what they needed; all her strength, passion and ingenuity. They worshipped her, and crowded around her to touch her skirt and kiss her hand. She was their heroine, and beloved mother.

Eight

Ascended Masters 1987

One day while at Krotona, Sylvia recommended I give a copy of my writings to the head of Krotona to see what he thought of it—"Maybe he could help you get it published!" she exclaimed. So I gave Sylvia a copy of the chapters I had, and she handed them on to him, and set a day for me to go see him.

Today was that day. As I walked through the main hall to get to his office I wasn't as nervous as I thought I'd be—in fact I was proud. I loved Annie, and hoped that came across in the writing. I knocked on the outside door of his office. *What an honor it was to have an appointment to meet with the President of the Theosophical Society at*

Krotona! I must act confident, I thought. I knocked again. It was very quiet. I tried to look through the window of his study, but a frayed curtain blocked most of the view.

He must be here—I knocked again, no answer. I'll wait. I turned around and gazed at the portico and courtyard garden. His office was connected to the arched entranceway to the library and Great Hall. Blue hydrangeas framed the stucco walls, and a large terra cotta fountain overflowed and splashed with noisy water. A hummingbird darted in front of the door; its buzz startled me.

"Come in, my dear! So sorry to keep you waiting!" An elderly man opened the door and motioned me to sit—I walked across the oriental carpet and sat where he pointed. "I just finished your manuscript this morning; it's lovely, and so….poignant." I took a breath. "Oh, and please just call me Felix."

Felix was a tall thin gentleman, handsome, and dressed in an old style dark suit that made him look as if he had just stepped out of the 1800's. I liked him the minute I saw him, and when he opened his mouth to speak I liked him even more. He had a soft voice, with a slight British accent and he spoke slowly. I could tell he was accustomed to being listened to—but today he was going to listen to me as well. I hoped my voice wouldn't tremble.

Felix sat himself down behind an antique desk on which was the original copy of my manuscript—the first few chapters of the narrative of Annie's life. I waited for him to speak first.

"I've always been terribly fond of Annie Besant," he said, "and I think you've done her justice here." He lifted up the papers. "I can tell from your writing that you are fond of her as well."

"I am. I feel as if I've been called to do this writing on her life." *Should I tell him the astrological synchronicity? Probably not.*

"That's a good sign to feel a call." He paused, then leaned forward towards me, tapping his chest. "She's in here, very deeply." His milky blue eyes glistened as though he was almost looking through a veil. "I don't think most people know her in the way we do."

And then I did it—I told him the whole story about finding her books, the similarities in the astrological charts, what the psychic had said, and our move across country from Rhode Island to California. When I get nervous I tend to talk too much.

But the more I talked the more his eyes widened and a smiling curious expression came across his face—

"You even look a little like her," he said, "and, you have her courage; the willingness to drop everything and open up a new chapter in your life. I suggest you send this to our publishing house as soon as you're done. I'm sure they'll want to publish it."

I took a deep breath and every muscle in my body relaxed. "Thank you," I replied, realizing I wasn't going to have to explain and plead my case.

He sat back in his chair and looked out his window through the frayed silk curtain. "Have you researched in the library here? You could browse among some of the older and lesser known books?"

"I'd love that; there's still so much I don't know. And I haven't written a bibliography yet." I finally allowed myself to look around the room, my eyes lingering on two framed drawings of rather serious looking men on either side of his desk. They looked like prints I'd seen of Jesus once. "Do you mind telling me who they are?" I asked, pointing to the prints.

He smiled. "Yes, they're part of what you don't know. And, you must be aware that Krotona is the esoteric section of the Society—the part of the Society that is about helping people like you get in touch with them…if you're ready." He coughed, a deep uneasy cough, but kept going: "Esoteric Theosophy is about the path of discipleship—about connecting with the Ascended Masters." He took a deep breath.

"I know very little about that. But I do remember HPB said she met with some Masters living in Tibet when she was young, and she continued receiving teachings from them, later… as a medium."

He nodded his head. "You've got it right. Annie also received messages from Master Morya—that's him here." He pointed to one of the prints. "There are lots of Ascended Masters of the Great White Brotherhood—and I say 'white' because they work through white magic not black magic—and Jesus, Buddha, Kwan Yin…they're a part of it too. Wise ones we'll meet on the other side someday."

Felix picked up a string of mala prayer beads on his desk and started fingering them. "What people don't understand is that we can raise our vibrations to communicate with the Masters. Some people say it's a rigorous path; no meat, tobacco, or alcohol of course, and meditation of a certain kind."

I nodded my head too, but this was all news to me. "And who's the other Master?" I asked.

"That's Master Kuthumi here, and Master Morya there." He stood up and took a book off his shelf and brought it to me. "You'll find this one at the library; it's about them." I read the title: "The Mahatma Letters" by A.P. Sinnett.

He stood over me. "And I see you haven't written about one of ours: Krishnamurti? You're not up to that part of the story yet…"

He was putting me on the spot with that question. "Was he one of yours…ours?" I asked, not so innocently, knowing that many—if not most—Theosophists didn't consider him one of theirs anymore.

"He was—he was discovered and raised by us." Felix sat down again. "But he didn't like the rites and rituals and initiations; understandable for a young man. Yes, he rejected us, but the message he brought to the world was good—he took the path of the mystic, whereas we are occultists. So there are differences."

"But he never rejected Annie." I added. "And maybe there are many paths up the mountain." I said, knowing that we would be disagreeing with Krishnamurti, if he was sitting in the room with us. "Of course, he'd say Truth is a pathless land."

We both laughed, and our conversation meandered, till finally Felix extended his hand to me. "Thanks for coming, Elizabeth. Send these chapters in; what I see is excellent. I'm sure it will be accepted. And good luck, with everything."

What a pleasure it had been to meet this wise Soul. I went to the library right after our meeting, and left with my arms overflowing with books, and my heart full with joy.

Six weeks later I received a letter of rejection from the Theosophical Publishing Press. They were kind enough to encourage my writing and to add that although many of them liked the book in progress, a member of the publishing house had found my bibliography to be at fault. One man on the committee said I was getting information from "faulty sources" that would reflect negatively on the Society.

This one person stopped the manuscript from being published. I would not accept their restriction of my research; there would be other publishers, but to be rejected by Annie's Society cut deep into my heart.

I never told Felix what happened; he had been so encouraging. In fact, he died not long after our visit. I wondered if he would now be joining with the other Masters he so loved; he seemed to me to be a Master in this life. But what did I know? I only knew he was now "on the Other Side" and would now be someone I could approach in meditation. Maybe he could help get Annie's story out into the world.

Nine

You Can Do What You Think You Can't Do

Rejection. That's a hard word to swallow. And a rejection because someone didn't like my book sources! That made me angry—but anger is often better than sadness, and certainly better than giving up in defeat. I remembered Annie once said that one should always know all sides to an issue or situation before taking a stand. If she were me, she would have read *all the books*, not just the ones that kept to the accepted version. But those publishers weren't going to allow me to do that; they obviously didn't trust my judgment.

However I wasn't completely disappointed because I was beginning to have second thoughts. As I wrote Annie's story, images of her meeting Madame Blavatsky, the match-girls strike, and her life in India began forming into *a movie* in my head. Here was such visually rich material and I was telling it like a narrator in an old-fashioned biography! *This could be a movie! Why am I telling the story this way?* I thought.

I ran into the kitchen and saw Harry reading the newspaper. I threw my writing papers down on the table in front of him. "This should be a movie! But I don't know how to do it—how to write a screenplay!"

Harry looked up from his reading, and pointed his finger right at me. "You could learn—we are here right in the heart of screenplay country. Everyone I run into here is writing a movie. You could too."

I sighed, thinking…*another big project but I could do it, if I wanted. Did I want to take on learning a new skill? Not really, but I could try! Maybe this is what Annie would want…it would have lots of visuals like a book at first, and have lots of dialogue—the bones of a screenplay.*

"So, do you have any books on screenwriting?" I asked the guy at the bookstore on Ojai Avenue.

He led me to a section of books on writing, and then to the screenplay shelf. "Take your pick, they're all great. I think everyone is buying them because of the contest."

"What contest?" I asked.

"*The Santa Barbara Screenwriters Guild Contest*. It's huge." He looked at me, tilting his head, giving me a big flirty grin. "You should enter it. I can tell you've got a movie in you." He laughed and pointed to the poster on the bulletin board. "You haven't got much time. But hey, that's enough if you know what you're doing."

What a salesman, I thought, as I handed him the money for the last 3 books on the shelf. Then I raced home to begin reading… and writing in my new style. It wasn't easy.

"I can't do this Harry." I said pointed to my new books on the craft. "The screenplay style is so stiff and limiting. You have to type each character's name on a separate line from the dialogue…and any description has to be done in a certain way with the camera in mind. It's hard to write, because you're so limited—I tried it."

"Don't use that form then!" He shook his head. "At least not at first. Why don't you write it like a book with a lot of dialogue—as if it were a movie unfolding in your head, a story with scenes, and then *later transpose* it into screenplay form?" Harry grinned. "Just get it down, like a first draft; just do it."

I stared at him knowing he had said exactly what I needed to hear. "You are amazing, honey." I kissed him; one long sweet and delicate kiss. "I am so blessed," I told him, as I whipped myself around and took off for my writing room.

I was hoping he'd make dinner that night so I could jump right into this new project.

Instead the phone rang. It was my mother. Should I answer it or not? This wasn't her usual time to call; she preferred calling first thing in the morning, so I should answer it, just in case it was an emergency. I starred at the phone ringing knowing that this could deplete my evening's energy for work—but what if—what if she was ill? What if it was serious? I picked up--

"How are you Mom?" That's always a bad way to start a conversation with someone who's clinically depressed.

She explained in some detail exactly what was wrong, where, why, and how. It mostly came down to the fact that Harry and I weren't there to fix things. And then it began…

"How could you leave me like this? Will I ever see you again?" she whined. I reminded her that she had come to visit a few months ago and had a wonderful time. Then I suggested she come out for Christmas even though the contest deadline was Jan 15th. Why did I say that? How could I do that?

She unhappily agreed that she would probably need to come to visit me, as we weren't all going to come see her. I agreed. I said that a little vacation would probably be good for her; she suggested that I should call her more often as she had no friends or relatives…I asked about the relatives that I knew she had and her few friendships, but she sighed, and said I didn't understand.

"They don't mean anything to me," she pleaded. "I don't understand you, Janet, I don't understand how you can do this to me!"

"Do what to you?" I asked.

"Leave me here…to die. You just don't care." This was the beginning. And so it went for the next half hour till Harry called me for dinner. I'd lost my appetite by then and only wanted to cry.

The next morning I struggled with the screenplay form. It seemed too skeletal; boring. I lay down on the couch and covered my eyes with the eye pillow; drew a blanket up around me, and wondered why I was feeling so miserable. Writing has its ups and downs like any creative work, but why this despair? The brick wall was there; I'd lost any way around it. I couldn't continue because I didn't know the right way to tell the story. Most of all, I was sure no one would find it, read it or like it.

But maybe that wasn't true; something else felt off; was I struggling with being dishonest? I worried that if I wrote honestly I would say things that the Theosophists and the "Krishnamurti people" wouldn't like; that Annie and Krishnamurti had human flaws. But I wasn't going to defame these people; but to simply tell my own experience with them.

The "Hollywood screenwriting people" would say: *who are these people anyway and who cares?* Could I make them care? They would like it to be drenched in exaggerated drama; *a little more sex and violence please*, they'd say. No matter how I wrote it, some people would approve, and some would nit-pick it for errors. I'd better get thick skinned! Could I bend my will and be more constrained or outrageous in my writing? Wouldn't I feel duplicitous? Yes. My Libra indecisiveness had to find a middle way that was honest: I had to write the book-screenplay as I found the Truth.

But why couldn't I even come up with a title? I was depressed...or going into depression; I could feel it in my body, in my nerves. Ridiculous!

And then it hit me. What was wrong was that there was no Annie collaborating with me! When I thought of Annie I would see her as the ultimate critic—her arms folded and looking like a stern headmistress waiting till I had written something she approved of—and I imagined that she didn't approve of anything yet. Maybe she didn't understand the concept of "first draft." I reminded myself that she was not a book reviewer nor the head of the Society now, just as Jesus was not the Pope at the Vatican. But still, I felt her presence as a withholding critical mother.

But she had promised to collaborate! Where was she now? Wasn't this the time when I most needed her? I pulled the blankets off me, got off the couch and went into my writing room and sat in front of my writing.

I closed my eyes, took a few deep breaths and laid my head down on the desk.

"Annie, you said you would collaborate, I need you now. I can't wait any longer." I could see Annie in my mind's eye, unfolding her arms and holding out her hands to me. I took them. I was sad. She put her arms around me.

I opened my eyes and stared at the large red and gold ring I'd found in a shop in Ojai yesterday morning. It was still right on my desk, as I had been taking it on and off yesterday, wondering if it was too big for my hand. And then I "heard her"—she said: *"Put the ring on."* I imagined her holding the ring and slipping it on the center finger on my right hand. *"That's the Saturn finger"* she said, *"and it gives concentration, discipline and commitment, but most of all, it will remind you that I am here. I am here for you and this work."*

I put the ring on; it reminded me of the ring Madame had given to Annie to wear; now it spoke to me of her promise that she was collaborating with me—in some way it was true. I was going to be a truth teller and she was going to help. Whether I noticed it or not, I believed she would be there. I wasn't expecting miracles.

However the next day, instead of having the writing just flowing, I stumbled along with it till about noon, at which time I began questioning myself, wondering whether Annie was helping me or not. She didn't say it would be easy, just that she would be there. What could I do? I cleaned my writing desk, arranged my papers and books, and finally sat back in the chair and began meditating.

"Annie, I need you." I prayed. "I can't do this by myself. I'm feeling sick over this." Then something shifted. I began to feel different; as if I could see her arms out, enfolding me. It felt good. And then again, it was as if I heard her words:

"*Imagine into it. Let me be with you as we relive the story together. Stay out of it a little bit; just listen…*" It was as if I was in a dream, and I could see a knowing smile come up over her normally serious face. At that moment I surrendered any resistance to doing my part.

After 5 hours of writing, I was in a strange and wonderful mood, but I needed a break. I walked the land and breathed in the scent of the orange blossoms in the orchard and the jasmine I had planted by the doorway. The shadows of the clouds were moving over the mountains flowing in patterns of dark and light, always undulating, like waves breaking on the shore.

It was getting towards dusk, and I thought how beautiful it might be to drive up to the Upper Ojai and go to the tree where I had been earlier; the spot where Annie had first seen the soaring valleys and mountains, the spot where I had created a little altar.

As I got out of the car I remembered the mandala-like earring of the two birds encircling each other that I'd left on my make-shift rock altar, and wondered if it was still there. Someone must have found and taken it by now.

I approached the spot reverently. I could see the little stone cairn, my altar, and there it was! My earring—still there, untouched! And around it were tokens left by people who had come to same spot…feathers, painted rocks, pieces of paper, Tibetan coins….who had left all of these? And who had left my token ring right in the middle of it all? It didn't matter.

This was an altar under Annie's tree, and it had been found and acknowledged as a sacred place.

I walked around the altar for a moment, wondering what to do. Then I sat down. I would meditate—just simple breathing, and clearing my mind. And the more I breathed the more I wanted to conjure up Annie or anyone on the 'Other Side." But what I felt instead, was a "strengthening" inside of me and the image of a light going down a vertical axis through the center of me. It only lasted for a moment and then was gone.

As I drove home I wondered if this "strengthening and light" was a way that we ourselves can become like the "Masters." Maybe they are simply ordinary people who have tuned into this frequency and who, after death, choose to help others. I wasn't sure, but I certainly felt stronger, and the next day the writing flowed right into the story. It felt like I was getting help…

Ten

The Screenplay Visualized.

I can almost see the scene laid out before me...

London; 1889.

The interior of a Victorian bedroom: heavy curtains are drawn, letting in only a sliver of light. The room is typical of the upper class taste of the time, although the velvet green furniture looks distinctly worn and dusty. On the fireplace mantel a dimly lit oil lamp illuminates a collection of old family photographs.

Annie is in bed, unmoving, her face turned to the wall. An assortment of medicine bottles and untouched food is on a table beside her. Tacked up on the wall is the front page of the

Pall Mall Gazette on which her name appears in large letters next to an article on "The Match Girl's Strike."

Muffled voices are heard fighting outside the door, until the door is thrust open and there stands a large imposing looking woman, with an exasperated housekeeper: "I told her you were not seeing anyone!"

"Let her in." Annie rasped, her cold being as bad as her depression.

The 200+ pound woman, Madam Blavatsky, lumbers into Annie's room. She is dressed in dark silks and brocades and carrying a huge hard-bound book under her arm. Her round head is covered by a thin black shawl. She extends her hand and speaks in a deep Russian accent.

"Helena Petrovna Blavatsky… my dear Mrs. Besant, for so long I have wished to meet you…" She took a breath.

Annie turned over and extended her hand. Madame held it for too long. Annie pulled her hand back and stared at the wall. She saw Madame surveying the room, noticing the untouched food.

"You're not eating!" she looked around with disgust. Annie could see what she saw; a dismal sickroom—but Madame didn't know she'd been dwelling in the land of her grief and anger, rather than the condition of her lungs.

At the moment she burst into the room Annie was thinking about her brother, and wondering why he always had been the one to be on the receiving end of most of her mother's love. Since mother's death she hadn't heard from him. She was wallowing in self-pity about everything, but mostly angry at God. God wasn't there for her or anyone else. With what she'd seen, she'd become an atheist.

Annie roused herself, letting the words tumble out: "Please…go away. I saw you there in the courtroom that day; you know it all; and, I *know* who you are."

Madame sniffed, her neck arching. "I saw a woman with great courage there; a woman ahead of her time. What do those *men* in the courtroom know?"

Annie turned her face back to Madame. "What do *you* know?"

"I know whatever I need to know; I get my orders from the Masters."

"I'm sorry, Madam Blavatsky, but I don't believe in spiritualism, or you, or Theo-so-phy or whatever you call it." She struggled to sit up.

Madame jabbed her hand in the air: "No need to believe. You have to experience! Your life is of no use to anyone now! Look at you! Do you know you have a destiny to fulfill? So what's all this?" Her hand waved across the room in disgust. "Flapdoodle! You are going to be a victim now? Rot away in this room? You think this is what you were meant for?"

Annie said nothing. Madame's protruding eyes pierced her to the quick. She felt ashamed.

Madame leaned over the bed, too close to her face and whispered: "Sometimes…you have to fail in the eyes of the world first…"

"Oh I fail, and I can *seem to win*, but inside… I've failed. Nothing makes sense anymore." She sat up.

"It's because you don't have any idea how it all fits together! One day you're picketing the factories and writing letters to the big wigs to squeeze a shilling out of them for the girls--" She lumbered over to the newspaper headlines of the Match Girls Annie had hung on the wall and pulled it down, sticking it under her nose.

"And then you see these girls slapping their children around, drinking, having more children…eh? And you, you're writing books for them about how *not* to have more babies---yes? Then you collapse in despair because nothing seems to change. Am I right?"

"You're right." Annie said. It was uncanny how Madame knew exactly what was bothering her—after the strike Annie had seen one of the match girls on the street hitting her child and yelling profanities.

Annie sighed: "When I was a minister's wife I saw the appalling conditions that the poor live under—mothers, worn out by constant childbearing—living without enough food or the minimal comforts of life...these women have no dignity left! And what we can do is so small, so insignificant it seems to barely make a difference."

She coughed and blew her nose. "But they took my children away! They said I was an *unfit mother!*"

"You don't know your worth." Madame stood up and started moving about the room again. "I've been following your life in the papers for years. You are an extraordinary woman!" Spotting a photograph she picked it up; it was an old daguerreotype of Annie's mother. Madame took it off the mantel and handed it to Annie.

"Open it," she demanded.

"No!—what right have you—this is my mother!" She took it out of Madame's hands.

"Yes, I know. Please, just read me what's behind the photograph." She leaned over and her large protruding eyes bore into Annie again.

"How do you know something's behind here?" Annie's fingers caressed her mother's image; then she stuck her nail between the glass and frame and tried to extract what had been hidden there.

Madame picked up a letter opener from the night table—and swaying it like a long elegant knife, she made a sword-like gesture mimicking a queen handing a sword to her knight.

Annie reluctantly pried open the back of the daguerreotype and unraveled the old letter. "Dearest Mama…" She stopped.

Madame tilted her head. "Go on…go on—just the last paragraph."

Annie coughed. What choice did she have? "An imperious necessity forces me to speak the Truth as I see it, whether the speech please or displease, whether it brings praise or blame. That one loyalty to Truth I must keep whatever friendships fail me or human ties be broken…"

"Go on. Go on!" Madame insisted.

"…for when it is my time to go, dearest Mama, I ask no other epitaph for my tomb than "She tried to follow Truth."

"That's it! 'A noble person, for a noble cause.' I have need of you, Mrs. Besant. Please, come see me." She reached into her bag and handed Annie her card. Then she handed her the book she'd been holding, *The Secret Doctrine.* "Come see me when you finish it! I do hope you might want to review it for your newspaper."

When she left Annie opened the book and read: *"The eternal parent wrapped in her ever invisible robes had slumbered once again for seven eternities..."* She groaned, and picked up a copy of "The Times" from the other side of her bed and went to the book reviews: *"The Secret Doctrine, written by the Russian aristocrat, Madame Blavatsky, is unreadable and incomprehensible—it is choked to death by vast quantities of indigestible materials."*

"Hah! I thought so." she said aloud to no one, and turned up the wick on the oil lamp. She brought the newspaper up to her nose again and read aloud some more: *"Madame Blavatsky's Theosophy is the esoteric basis of all religions. It has no dogmas, other than the belief in the essential brotherhood of all. Its members are devoted to the study of comparative religion and investigating the unexplained laws of nature."*

Nothing wrong with that, in fact it sounded interesting she thought. So she continued: *"Although subscribing to no formal creed, most Theosophists accept the doctrines of reincarnation and karma, and carry a belief of non-violence which extends to all creatures, both human and animal."*

Annie watched the flickering light from the oil lamp for a few minutes then walked over to her desk and sat down. She began writing: *"For most readers, the study of this book will begin in bewilderment and end in despair..."* Little did she know that this was *not* how it would be for her. The next day she began reading in earnest, and then she began writing. Before long *The Pall Mall Gazette* would have a glowing review of *The Secret Doctrine* by Annie Besant.

Eleven

Madame Helena Petrovna Blavatsky

Madame Blavatsky's House: 17 Lansdowne Road, London.

Annie knocked on the imposing door. A formal unsmiling man answered; he was tall, bearded, and dressed in a black suit with an amethyst cross hanging from his neck.

"Good morning. I'm here to see Madame Blavatsky."

"Your name?"

"Annie Besant."

He led her into a dimly lit, smoky room. Her eyes swept over the abundance of oriental antiques and objects: Japanese cabinets, ornate armoires, fans, an antique samovar, and a golden Buddha near the fireplace. On the other side of the room was a collection of 'taxidermies': a lionesses' head over the door, monkeys peering out of nooks, stuffed birds perched on bookcases. But the grandest spectacle was a large baboon, standing upright, dressed in a fancy dress coat and tie, holding Darwin's book *The Origin of Species* under its arm.

The man left Annie in this room standing directly opposite the baboon. She dropped her heavy bag on the floor and walked over to the baboon and stared it down, eye to eye. A smile began to creep up Annie's face as she slid Darwin's book out of the baboon's grasp.

"So tell me ole beast—are we cut from the same cloth?" she asked him, as she took Madame's book out of her bag and slipped it into his hand. She would show Madame that she had a little humor, and wouldn't be intimidated.

Madame rushed in, spotting Annie next to the baboon: "So would you agree with me, Mrs. Besant, that the Darwinists proved nothing with their materialistic science?"

"I don't know what I believe just now, Madame. But I *try* to see myself as a most *reasonable* woman!" Now face to face, Annie pulled Madame's *Secret Doctrine* back from the baboon's grasp. She grinned and handed the book to Madame.

Madame's mouth fell open. "What unbelievable gall you have!" They both laughed. Madame lit up a cigarette and slowly exhaled the smoke creating a screen between their faces. "You don't understand the folly of science as opposed to the world of the spirit, do you?"

"No, I suppose not." Annie replied. Madame drew deeply on her cigarette again and frowned.

"There's a lot of wisdom in your book, Madame Helena," Annie said, gathering her courage: "Your ideas of divine justice and the Soul's journey soothed me deeply. And….I didn't come here to play games. I'm sorry—I just wasn't expecting to see a baboon. I'm here because I want to know more of what you believe."

Madame said nothing, but moved over to the large antique samovar, poured some black tea, and brought two thin china cups back to a black lacquered table. She motioned Annie to sit in a delicate chair next to the table.

Sitting herself in a larger chair she began: "I believe….that is, Theosophists believe, in the mystical core of all religions; the perennial philosophy, which is the core mystical truth in each religion." She pointed around the room: "There is much theatre in religion—*but there is no religion higher than Truth.*"

Annie nodded her head and noted the change of tone in Madame's voice. She was getting serious. "But perhaps you…Theosophists… think you have a little corner on that Truth?"

"Mrs. Besant, you're the one with the newsmagazine of that name, '*My Corner*', not me. But please, forgive me my rudeness or impatience. My dear, I've been waiting so long for you…you don't know how much I need you."

Annie was taken aback by that comment, but managed to continue, pointing to Madame's book: "I'm here because these ideas of karma and reincarnation that you write about in the *Secret Doctrine*…at such great length…they interest me—no—more than that; they're the only ideas that make sense to me."

Madame smiled and wiped a napkin across her moist forehead. Then she yelled out:

"Charles! Come here." The bearded man walked in and stood by Madame's side. "Annie Besant, this is Charles Leadbeater. I think you two might have some work to do together. Charles is, as they say, my right hand man."

They nodded politely as Madame continued her introduction: "Annie Besant, is a passionate and brilliant woman—a worker, a reformer, a leader." He nodded.

Annie waited to see if he would say anything but he just looked at her. "Nice to meet you," she whispered, and turned her head back to Madame: "It makes sense to me that reincarnating Souls would go through hard lives till they've learned the lessons they needed to learn, and then there would be some kind of Divine Justice later in this life or another." Annie laughed nervously. "I'm giving your book a good review for the paper, but everyone thinks I've gone mad."

Madame sighed and touched Annie's knee with her hand. "I know. That's what I like about you."

Annie dived in again: "But I think your book, if you don't mind my saying, attaches too much importance to karma and fate, and too little importance to the power of free will! Don't we make our own destiny?"

"Oh, we do that, indeed! Fate plus free will equals destiny. Hmm…so you think you might believe in the Divine Laws of the Universe? That's nice." Madame took a long sip of tea and her voice lowered: "So tell me then, was it Divine Justice that took your children away? You see, it's a little more complicated. It doesn't always work out in one life."

"Was it Divine Justice that—labeled you a fraud?" Annie sputtered. "The '*Committee for Psychic Research*' has said that, but I don't agree, of course."

"You think I don't know about that?" Madame stirred her tea, and for a moment she looked scared, like a trapped animal. Then she tilted her head as if she was trying to listen to something. She put a finger to her lips motioning to Annie to be quiet.

"I understand." She said to no one, and then reached into her pocket and drew out a pack of playing cards and started quickly shuffling them. She laid the pack on the table and turned one over.

"Queen of Spades...hm...not an easy life; one steeped in illusions and disillusions...and hard choices. A life with many chapters." She looked up at Charles and then back at Annie. "That's you."

Annie reached over and pulled a card out of Madame's hand and laid it down on top of the other: "Queen of Hearts!" she exclaimed. "My choice—my free will."

"Excellent choice, my dear"! Madame crooned.

She looked up at Charles. "Pick one!"

He picked a card and laid it on top. It's was the Joker. Madame and Annie laughed, but Charles didn't; he flipped over another card: the King of Hearts."

"My goodness, one never knows..." Madame chuckled, then her face turned serious as she leaned across the table: "My dear, would you honor us by coming back this next Tuesday night? We're having a gathering of a few people from our larger membership-you'll know a few; Yeats will be coming, and Oscar Wilde, and a few others who will be important in years to come. I do wish you'd be there too."

"Is this a séance? I don't know."

"Oh no, no, Mrs. Besant. I can tell you right now you have nothing to fear. But I have a great need for you. I have thought about you at length…I'm a reluctant believer myself!" She smiled. "However, the Masters have told me that you have important work to do for us."

"But I don't know…"

"Of course you don't know my dear! But they do." Madame slipped the veil off her head and grasped Annie's two hands in hers. "I don't know everything. But I take my orders as I'm given them." She looked up at the high ceiling and paused. "They have a use for you, and so…I need you. They say I won't be around much longer."

Annie covered her mouth with her hand and drew back. "I won't be used as a pawn, Madame, but let me think about this."

"A pawn? I thought of you as the Queen!" Madame exclaimed, though her face had the look of a Cheshire cat.

Twelve

Madame's Séance.

Madame's parlor. Evening.

The air was thick with pipe smoke and incense. Annie could see several porters hurrying about as they served Madame's black tea and vodka. In front of the fireplace, Madame appeared to be holding court with a circle of Theosophists cocooned around her, while Charles was standing in the rear observing the scene. He started walking over to Annie, but stopped as he saw a young Indian man approach her.

The Indian was short with a delightful countenance. "I've followed your reviews of the *Secret Doctrine* with great interest, Mrs. Besant.

Quite fascinating, don't you think? And the newspapers are full of news about you as well."

"Yes, they seem to find me an easy target for their attacks."

"They do. Easier to weave cotton…than to fight a battle, but in your case, I would say you must simply follow your way, your dharma. You have a calling, I suspect."

Annie was surprised by him saying she had a "calling" when she was feeling so lost, and without a calling or *dharma.* She didn't know how to respond—but just then Madame's cuckoo clock loudly chimed forth as if underscoring his words.

Was this a synchronistic sign or moment? Madame had told her to watch for these synchronicities, but she barely understood what she meant--something about an outer event echoing an inner feeling—could it be as simple as the loud clock and this strange little man's assessment of her? Madame said synchronicities meant something was important—for a moment a hush descended on the room till Madame uttered back to the clock an obnoxious—"Damn you!"

Annie was embarrassed, yet turned back to the Indian. "It's a good idea to look beyond the surfaces of things, don't you agree, Mr.---?"

"Gandhi. I'm not a regular here, just a student of law, visiting. And yes, I always do look beyond the obvious."

Just then, Madame spotted Gandhi. She strode across the room and shook his hands with great formality. Although Annie was standing right there, it was if she were invisible for the moment.

"Mr. Gandhi! I didn't notice you come in," she exclaimed.

"Your writings have aroused my curiosity" he smiled.

"Oh, really? Well I hope we don't disappoint you!" Madame stared at him intensely for a moment, and then turned around and retrieved a book from her bookshelf and handed it to him.

"So Mr. Gandhi, have you taken the time to read the *Bhagavad-Gita*? Or has your English law education robbed you of interest in your heritage?"

"I'm ashamed to say I haven't read it." He held the book reverently.

"This should be most enlightening to you, my young man." Gandhi bowed slightly and smiled sheepishly as Madame sat down and lit up a cigarette. As her adoring court resumed their place around her, he seemed to slip away unnoticed in the crowd.

Charles headed towards Annie. "Pleased to see you came tonight, Mrs. Besant." He was beaming, and looked excited.

"I was a little late. Did I miss anything?"

Charles laughed, and pulled over some chairs to sit on. "She always says so much, but she did say one thing that was most strange. She said America will be the birthplace of the New Age!"

"America? I wonder why? And when is this New Age?"

"She didn't say. But she's got something on her mind; I can tell." He raised his eyebrows and gave Annie a "knowing" look.

"Must you stare at me like that?" Annie said, frowning.

"I was intrigued by the thought forms you were putting out. Do you always resist so much? Perhaps anger isn't such a bad defense against so much sadness…yes?"

"How do you assume to know these things?"

He pulled at his beard thoughtfully. "You were often angry with me in our last life too."

"Oh really? Angry at you? Why?"

"And even more at yourself. You had high expectations of everyone." So apparently he could see into the past as well as being clairvoyant. The conversation came to a halt as the poet, Yeats, arrived with Oscar Wilde. They were making their way over to the tea table, as the noise in the room started to drown out the quieter conversations.

Yeats began talking loudly and struggling to get Wilde's attention: "I'm very curious if there are Masters living in Tibet who care about us... or maybe they've passed on to the Other Side. Maybe they're like muses; the origin of *inspiration*." Yeats looked reflective.

Oscar Wilde looked anything but reflective. "Perhaps there's a Master who is your muse; though I must say I'm not feeling very inspired these days." Wilde's eyes were wandering, seemingly more intrigued by a svelte young porter walking by, than talking to Yeats. He looked with dismay at the hors d'oeuvres—and swept his hand across the food table: "If this is the way the Queen treats her subjects, she doesn't deserve to have any!"

Just then Madame's voice rose up over the noisy din, complaining in her Russian accent: "It's mostly flapdoodle I tell you! Half the world are idiots and the other half, cynics! They must have these phenomena—these miracles—or they won't believe a thing. But...but the purpose of this Society is to prepare humanity for the reception of a World Teacher! People must understand that....they must understand...." Her words trailed away.

Yeats leaned into Wilde's ear. "She's told me it's all about putting oneself in conscious alignment with the Master..."

Wilde roared: "With who? Master Leadbeater? Hah! *And what rough beast, its hour come round at last, slouches towards Bethlehem to be born?*"

"That's quite eloquent, Wilde, mind if I write it down?" Yeats took out a notebook and scribbled down the words.

The cuckoo clock chimed forth yet again, this time in eleven resounding calls. A loud moan came from Madame, and then she fell to the floor. Charles rushed to lift her; her eyes were fluttering open and closed. "Yes, Yes…I understand!" She spoke breathlessly while pointing to Annie and Charles.

"They're saying—you two—you must find the one who will be the avatar for the New Age! You must go to India to find him; the great spiritual Teacher. It will be …like the second coming….of the Christ. He will be Maitreya himself."

All eyes turned on Annie. "Me, Madame? How would I even know him?"

Madame's head tilted to the side the way she did when she was listening to *them*. She spoke haltingly: "He will call you by name; your rightful name. He will call you 'Mother' in Hindi: 'Amma.' Charles will help. He will know him, when he sees him."

Madame then pulled off her large ring and held it out to Annie. "Take this! Take it!" She held a deep red ring with occult symbols on it up to Annie.

Annie stood there speechless, while Madame held out the ring, her hand trembling.

In a raspy voice she went on: "The ring holds a legacy. We all come and go, but this—here—shows the marks of the one unbroken life of the Soul." She paused, her lips quivered, her eyes were glazed and red. A look of sad vulnerability come over her as she touched Annie's hand. "I want you to have it, my dear."

The ring represented the lineage of her Theosophical Society, and by accepting it Annie would be making a commitment to carry on her work, or at least to go to India to try to find this boy; the new Spiritual Teacher.

Annie's words tumbled out: "I don't know—I don't know if I can make a commitment to what you have in mind..."

"Look at me. I'm not going to be around much longer. Do you understand? If you are trying to follow Truth, then consider. You know this is the closest thing you've found to Truth. And I tell you, you have been called. This is meant to be."

There was silence in the room. All eyes were on Annie. Slowly, like a bride to her groom, she held out her hand to Madame as she slid the ring onto Annie's finger. Madame's head fell backwards, as Leadbeater reached into his side pocket, and placed some pills into her mouth. Then he started fanning her with the nearest oriental fan.

"She'll be fine." He said, and then he yelled to the stunned group: "Go home! It's *over.* Over!" He looked not only agitated, but rather annoyed.

Annie took Madame's hand for a moment, then whispered something in Madame's ear and dismissed herself.

Thirteen

Miracles Among the English

Annie is sitting at a desk, reading aloud to herself, a letter she has just written.

"My dearest daughter, Mabel, and finest son, Digby~

I do hope you two are doing well and getting along better with your father. You know he is doing the best he can, so you need to follow his advice, although in matters of the heart, you can always be private. I can imagine how hard it is for you to understand all that has happened in the past and I hope your hearts always remain open and understanding. How is your schooling going? Are you liking Papa's new parish?

In the last letter I told you a bit about meeting Madame Blavatsky, and now there's more to tell. She's calling me to work for her Society and although I'm somewhat reluctant, I'm going to take up the position she has offered me. My days in the courts and on the streets are over—at least for now. I hope you'll understand.

And I want you to understand more—because you will hear about her, and perhaps me, and you know how the newspapers love to mock people. I have not lost all my marbles in doing this, but she's not an easy woman to understand because she seems both full of wisdom and—dare I say magic? It's up to each of us to decide what we believe or not. I'm not going to tell you what to think, only that I know you will hear from your father and others that she's a fraud. I don't believe that, although I don't understand how or why she does these things!

For me, it's all about the wonderful spiritual ideals she has for her Society and the great ancient truths of karma, reincarnation and divine justice. But that's a longer letter or talk. Let me tell you how I observed some of her "magic." I wrote everything that happened in my journal right after it happened so I wouldn't forget, and now I can share that with you~

Last Tuesday she invited me and about twenty other women to come for a luncheon, to be held outside in the lush gardens of an acquaintance of hers, Mrs. Geraldine Nettleton. Most of them were not a part of Madame's Society but we were all curious about her. After the meal was served, we all lingered under the dining tent pretending nothing was going to happen, but everyone was hoping for one of her famous "phenomena" to occur—these miracles (or magic) that she's become famous for creating.

I was feeling very much the observer, finishing the little meal, till I glanced over at Madame and saw her eyes closed. Nobody was looking at her then; it was if she had retreated. She had an air of total silence about her, and something about her stillness gave me a little shiver. Then I saw her lips tighten into a thin line of satisfaction.

"Start digging here--" she demanded to a young Indian porter. He looked surprised. We all wondered if this was going to be the time for "it" to happen, although we had no idea what "it" could be.

"—underneath that tree." Madame pointed with one finger, her hand waving a long cigarette holder like a wand. "Find a knife to cut through the grass and roots, and a couple of forks, and dig there. You will find it there." Nobody knew what "it" was, but the porter just did what he was told to do. Then Madame turned to our hostess, a dark haired young woman: "Now Geraldine, tell your friends here what happened to you last week—about your loss."

Geraldine gasped. Then she sputtered. "What I lost? How do you know what I lost? No one knows—I didn't tell you—!" Her eyes widened and she put her hand across her mouth. "It was an heirloom; handed down to me. It was my husband's Grandmother's brooch—I lost it; somehow." She covered her face in shame.

"You will have it back." Madame said as she looked at the porter. He began digging where Madame pointed. The rest of us sat in stunned silence as we looked at him digging away at the unbroken earth and grass beneath the tree. The porter's arms were elbow high in dirt by the time he looked up at us. He looked as confused as we were! "No, no…a little more to the right," she corrected herself. The porter did as he was told. Then we could see that he hit upon something; he pulled out of the ground a perfect ivory brooch.

He held it out to Geraldine. A loud sigh arouse from the group as Geraldine looked gratefully at Madame. She was now a believer. I didn't know Madame could do such things! And to see it before my very eyes was astounding.

But on our long slow retreat back to the main house, I dared to approach Madame. I mustered up every ounce of courage I had, and asked her: "How did you do that? Do you think it was fated today that you would know where the missing brooch was?"

"Fated?" She replied. "I do. It is my fate and my calling. It's not easy for me to risk my reputation doing these so called 'phenomena' but they must have these or they won't believe! And then they won't read my book—not that any of them would understand it. Bah! And I never know when I might fail."

She sighed, then turned to me and slipped her arm through mine as we walked ever so slowly; her large body lumbering along, leaning on me. "When we can make our minds be like still water, 'Beings' gather about us and we can do such things."

She pulled me closer to her and whispered: "Listening to the Master's voice is difficult…one must listen so deeply to get a vision….it takes a lot out of me." She wiped the moisture from her forehead, and looked at me with her sad protruding eyes. "Clairvoyance and these powers come once you can listen to the Masters—once you have understood deeply what it is you can do and must do. It is my karma to do this. I only wish I didn't have to create these miracles, these 'phenomena' or whatever they call them. But without them, they won't believe."

When I got home I opened her book, the *"Secret Doctrine"* again and began to read more. And the more I read, the more I believed; not everything, but there was *something* there that rang of Truth.

I have already given the book a good review for the newspaper, but this is a book that needs to be studied. I can't say I understand it completely, but the ideas of karma and reincarnation are the only things that make sense to me these days.

So my dear ones, maybe we will all understand these things someday, but for now I take it on faith, and hope you won't think badly of me for doing this—but I find Madame's sincerity with me breaking down any walls of disbelief I have.

And maybe someday there will be some divine justice for us, and we will spend time together again when you are older. I hope for that with all my heart. Till then, I will be going to India to work for a short time, and then I hope to be back in London around Christmas to see you both. Please don't worry about me, and I trust and pray you are well and continue to be well.

All blessings to you, and all my love,

Mama

Fourteen

Grave Decisions

Newspaper Headlines:

London Times: "Helena Petrovna Blavatsky, Russian spiritualist and spiritual leader of the Theosophical Society died suddenly at her home today in London at the age of 59. Leadership of the Society will be passed down to English social activist, Annie Besant.

New York Herald Tribune: "Blavatsky dies; young Hindu Being Sought as New World Teacher.

Graveside

A loud thump from a clod of earth is heard being thrown on a coffin. A large gathering of people have come together around her gravesite. Each one throws a handful of earth on the grave, but Annie is so distraught, her hand shaking so much, that the earth slips through her fingers. She is soon led away, leaning on the arm of Charles Leadbeater.

"When HPB died I felt I had lost not only my dearest teacher, but I was overwhelmed by the thought of carrying on her work. I wasn't a natural psychic such as she, and my fear might have overwhelmed me if I had not discovered the empowering effect of meditation. I endeavored to tune myself into the

higher power of the Universe and to watch for clues and signs around me. I still labored endlessly over my motives and searched for the threads of meaning in my life...but what held it all together was the idea of an ordered universe, of divine justice, as HPB had expressed it" (from *"An Autobiography"* by Annie Besant)

A small group of Theosophists stood around HPB's desk. Leadbeater was there. Annie's hand rested on a letter appointing her as Madame's successor and on her finger was Madame's red stone ring. Suddenly a prism of light bounced off the ring dazzling her eye.

At that moment, she stood up and proclaimed to those around her: "I will continue along the path that my spiritual mother has bequeathed to me."

Leadbeater smiled. "Good decision" he proclaimed.

The rest of the morning was a blur, but by the afternoon Annie had come to her senses and was surveying the large house. She found Leadbeater reading by himself in Madame's library.

He pointed to a chair and motioned her to sit. "I've been expecting you."

Annie smiled shyly and sat down.

"And I've been reading about how many of us have known each other in former lives. In fact, I did a meditation on you and looked into your past lives—have you ever heard of Hypatia? She was a Greek philosopher who was killed by a Christian mob for her pagan inclinations."

"Yes, I have...I've studied her. She was a brilliant woman who's been erased in history."

"How intuitive of you, my dear! Because you were her in one of your former lives."

"And you—who were you last time around?" Annie asked.

"At one time, I was in Greece, a student of Pythagoras. You were there as well."

Annie put her hands over her face. "This is overwhelming—I don't know about this.

But Hypatia was fascinating." She sighed and looked at his desk: there were scattered papers everywhere and a book called: *"The Chakras"* with his name on it as the author—and papers covered with pastel colored symbols and swirls. "What are these?" she asked.

"I'll show you. Would you like to try an experiment with me? Close your eyes..."

Annie closed her eyes, and folded her arms across her chest.

"Now I'm going to feel an emotion, and I want you to tell me what color you see ...and then we'll check your responses with my calculations here. If you allow your imagination to guide you, you'll see something. It's an ancient technique, called *kriyashakti*: it's a way to practice seeing *thought forms,* using imagination and intuition. Will you try it?"

Annie unfolded her arms. There was a long pause. "Green with a grey halo...now, rosy pink....blue swirls..."

"Beautiful. Perfect." He then took a carved wooden box out of the desk drawer and handed it to me. "These are the results of my experiments, like this, with Madame. We can do even more." He placed his hand over Annie's, his amethyst ring glinting in the light. "Now, we have much work to do together, my dear."

~

The light from his amethyst ring was the last clear memory she had, before she saw the light of India.

Fifteen

INDIA

"Are they going the right way Charles? Do they even know where the Theosophical Center is?" she shouted at Charles over the clamoring of the horses pulling the carriage; over the shrieks, shouts, bells, honks and heat of India. She wiped her face. She felt faint.

"The mansion—the estate is quite large, my dear, they know where it is." Charles looked calm. He always looked calm, but she saw he was rapidly fingering his mala prayer beads.

"I've never seen anything like this in my whole life! Look, Charles—the people just walk around the beggars like they weren't there! Even the British! Everyone is out on the street!" Just then they rounded a city corner to a somewhat quieter street. "What's that?" Annie pointed to a statue.

"What? Oh, yes...that's Kali, a Hindu Goddess. She's a powerful one—she's the dark side of the Mother; controlling, ruthless...yes, they worship her too. Nothing is excluded in India."

"They worship a woman with blood dripping down her face and skulls at her feet?"

"She's all over India. They honor the full range of human and God-like possibilities. You see, it's all One to them; even the bad mother. Kali sacrifices and destroys so that the new can be born."

"Why would anyone worship that?"

"No birth without death, my dear—symbolic, yes? You don't like it?" He had a perverse smile on his face. "The Soul, like Kali, is ruthless in its journey towards Truth. And she has integrity." He patted her hands.

"No, I don't like this." She withdrew her hands, and folded them in her lap.

"India hides nothing—pain, evil, intense beauty—it's going to get very hot here." Charles wiped his forehead with his handkerchief then looked at her: "You are so delightfully naïve at times! Is that why I'm so drawn to you? Hmm?"

She didn't look at him. Instead she took a deep breath and poked her head out of the carriage and yelled up to the driver. "Are the British helping the people here? I mean, it looks as if these people—the sick, the beggars—have been abandoned."

"Yes, Memsahib.

"Is that yes, they're being helped, or yes they're being abandoned?"

"Yes, Memsahib."

The driver just kept looking straight ahead, but she persisted: "Tell me, do you wish India was free of the British? Would they do better if they had home rule?"

Silence.

"Can you hear me?" Annie asked.

He turned around and looked at her with his dark eyes flashing. "Yes, Memsahib."

"Charles, maybe that's why I'm here—to help them."

"No, we have a destiny to fulfill here, have you forgotten? One way or another we will find *him*, and you must be willing to accept your role. I can see things others cannot. You must trust."

They pulled up to a white mansion surrounded by enormous trees. Suddenly all that could be heard were the sounds of birds cawing in the huge trees, as if announcing their arrival. They were ushered in to meet a stout man in a three piece suit, with spectacles and a long thick beard.

"Colonel Olcott! So good to see you again." Charles shook his hand vigorously. "And this is Mrs. Annie Besant, HPB's successor."

"So pleased to meet you, Mrs. Besant." He gave Annie a formal, if not forced, smile.

"Pleased to meet you." Annie replied. "I had no idea the Theosophical Society had such an imposing center. I mean it's quite beautiful."

"HPB and I bought this many years ago with the help of some members. She could never stand the climate though. Madame was always more suited—in temperament—to be our 'spiritual head' in London, while I've managed the administration from here."

"And quite well too, I'm sure." She looked around and could see some of Madame's

Madame exotic touches in the furnishings. "And we here by the direction of the Masters.... through Madame, of course... "

Olcott said nothing, but continued to look intently at her.

"...to find the boy."

"I've heard. Indeed, well he may be here. Who knows? Let me show you your rooms."

The cool air in the dark rooms was quite a contrast to the heat on the streets. A shiver ran through me. The bedroom was quite imposing with its high ceilings, its long sweeping curtains over one window and a few sparse but elegant furnishings.

Annie quickly undressed and climbed into the single bed. As she pulled up the light coverlet there was something warm and comforting about being in bed again; the comfort of a bed was always reassuring, even if it wasn't one's own bed. But as she lay there listening to the crickets, tossing and turning, her thoughts kept returning to her children. Oh, if only she could have tucked them into their beds tonight.

Sixteen

Finding Krishnamurti

"My dearest Mabel~

I do hope you are well and that your new Nanny and Father are helping you through these times. School can be hard, but I'm glad you're doing so well in your studies—and just give the mathematics some time. You'll get it. And... never forget how much I love you. Give Digby a hug from me, and ask him to write! You are so much better at correspondence than he is...I hope father hasn't turned him against me.

As for me; well, the heat here is so oppressive yet Charles and I go out every day to the villages looking for the boy. Tomorrow we are going to an orphanage, but I must confess feeling discouraged. The members here are skeptical of our mission, although Charles is impressing them with his clairvoyant powers and his ability to read auras. He says mine is dimming lately, and I don't doubt it, as I spend most of my time in my room when we're not out among the masses. Ah, I miss you.

Write more news of you! Sorry for this short letter; I just hope it gets off in the mail today.

All my love,

Mama"

Annie tucked the letter into the post basket outside the front door and decided to explore more of the estate. She walked through the foyer to the edge of the building and discovered a charming garden courtyard. Climbing pink and white roses crept up the stone walls and statues of cherubs and goddesses were everywhere. And there she was again—Kali—right in the center of the garden, next to a sunken pool.

"Charles?!" Annie almost jumped when she saw him. He was sitting next to a young Indian boy cutting his long black hair. The boy looked very thin.

"Annie! We were coming to see you in a few moments." He cut, combed, and stroked the boy's hair a little more. "I was just finishing his hair; so he would be more presentable to you. Well...so, here we are!" He turned the boy around to face her. He had beautiful features; but she couldn't tell if his eyes looked "vacant" or more like a mystery waiting to be explored.

"Mrs. Besant, this is young Krishnamurti—and those who love him call him, Krishnaji."

She bent down and shook his hand. "So pleased to meet you!" Annie smiled, and turned back to Charles. "This is him?"

Charles took her by the arm and led her a few feet away. "It is Him! His aura is totally golden. Pure. Not a shadow of hindrance or selfishness. I found him down by the river playing with some other boys yesterday. I've already spent some time with him."

"Are you sure?" she asked, incredulously.

Charles turned Annie to face Krishnaji again. "I am sure of this boy. Only Jesus himself had an aura this pure. Krishnaji, I'm going to leave you two, so you may talk." He turned to her again. "His father works here for the

Society. His English is remarkably decent, but his teeth will need to be fixed."

Krishnaji looked awkward and Annie wasn't sure what to do, till she spotted a stone bench by the edge of the small sunken pool. They sat down on it, and stared into the water looking at their reflections. Annie motioned for Charles to go away.

"Amma?" he said.

"What did you say?" Annie pulled back.

"Amma, I was wondering if you were going to be my mother now." Annie looked behind her to see that Charles had left.

"Tell me, did Mr. Leadbeater tell you to say that?

"To say what?"

"To say 'Amma'—please it's terribly important. Did he tell you to use that word, Amma?"

"No. I met Mr. Leadbeater yesterday morning, and he told me about Madame and the Masters and the prophecy—who I might be—"

"But why did you call me Amma just now?" she could almost hear Madame's voice in her head, saying she would know him because he would call her by this name.

"All I know…since I was a boy, I want to have my mother back. She died when I was young. And when I saw you just now, I felt—I don't know—but you feel to me like her. Are you going to be like her…my Amma?"

They stared at each other for a moment. "Perhaps. But do you want to do this? Do you think you're the One?" Annie asked.

"How can I know? I know only what I was told—that I was born in the holy room, the puja room; the 8th child of my family. The astrologer said there were unusual signs and that I would grow up to be special, and they named me after Sri Krishna. But how can I know?"

"Unusual astrological signs? They were… auspicious?"

He nodded his head shyly.

"If you are the One it will unfold. Madame taught that enlightenment is usually a process, not an instant knowing…unless you're a mystic." She looked at him curiously and then thought she must be making him uncomfortable.

"Well I am willing to be your Amma, Krishnaji. But that would mean I would adopt you, and send you to the best schools. In

England. But I will have to keep working for the Society, and traveling, but I could come see you….often. What do you think of that?"

"I must have my brother, Nitya, with me. We can come, but only together." He sounded like he knew what he wanted.

Annie nodded her head. "Krishnaji, you will never be forced to do anything you don't want to do...you understand?"

"Yes…but no. I don't know if I will grow up to be who you are looking for."

"You'll grow up to be whoever you really are meant to be...there will be signs." They leaned over the pool again and he looked like Narcissus looking at his image. It was then that she noticed a small notebook in his hand.

"What's this?" He held the book out to her. "May I read?" He nodded.

"At the Feet of the Master"--? Annie looked at the childish handwriting. It was signed by him. "You wrote this?"

"I think so. He tells me I did. Mr. Leadbeater and I…we went to the Masters last night. They tell me this—what's in here—and then I wrote it down first thing in the morning. It was like a dream…Mr. Leadbeater helped me with the words…and then, well, I forget."

She skimmed a few pages. "It's extraordinary! You did this?"

"I think so; yes."

"What do you mean, you think so? You went somewhere last night? And then you wrote it down."

"Yes. He said we went journeying on the astral plane. We met one of them."

She opened the little notebook again, and read a page, then another page, and then read aloud: "for wisdom is not memory, it is not knowledge, it is supreme openness to what is Real." She closed the notebook and handed it back to him, bowing slightly.

There was no way Annie could sleep that night. The sounds of the night chorus of insects were mesmerizing but the shock of the boy—and the book—was like adrenaline in her veins. This must be him! The little book was already a sign of his genius and wisdom.

He had a sense of mystery about him and innocence that she'd never seen before, and he'd already written something well beyond his years; though he looked to be only thirteen or fourteen years old.

Annie tossed and turned in her bed but sleep would not come. She could see the moon from her bedroom window and so decided to go back to the little courtyard where she met Krishnaji earlier. The hall was long, and as she passed by Charles's bedroom she heard voices. She stopped. Then she leaned in closer.

"Come..Krishnaji; it's good. Trust me. You must learn how to bring up the serpent! See… here…your hand on me, like this. Slowly, yes, that's right. Hold it…harder. You can do it now….come on my boy…you're shy…you don't understand. This is how you bring up the power—do it! That's it…harder…faster…keep it up!"

Annie buried her head in her hands, unmoving, gasping to breathe. With one last breath she burst into the room. Only the sheer white curtains, lit up by the moonlight, could be seen blowing through a window.

"Krishnaji, go back to your room!" she yelled. The two bodies moved on the bed, and Leadbeater stood up wrapping a blanket around him, while the boy reached for his robe. "That's right Krishnaji, put on your robe and go back to your room. It's OK. We'll talk later. Don't be afraid."

He walked by Annie, head down, while Charles approached, talking: "It's not your business, my dear. You don't understand this. It clears the chakras…males must do this. There are reasons why I need to teach him."

"Not like that! Shame on you! That's power over him! You're a weak man, Charles, you parade like a peacock but you don't choose one of your own kind…for this."

"You don't understand—boys have this pressure of sexuality—they must know how to relieve the tension."

"I don't need to understand more than what I heard with my own ears! You are to leave here tomorrow. I don't want to see you again!"

He grabbed her wrist. "You must not do this!" She wrestled herself away, and grabbed onto a chair.

"Come here! Sit down!" he threatened, grabbing the chair away from her, causing her to fall.

"Don't come near me!" she yelled. She got up and ran out the door, down the hall and outside into the courtyard. The moon had lit up everything, but the cobblestones were uneven. The stones tripped her feet. She put out her hands—and flew. She fell hard and the warm blood began trickling down her face and onto her hand.

Annie could see the statue of Kali not far from her, and with a groan, she dragged herself over and sat up beneath her. She crossed her legs and sat upright, in yoga position. Her dress was torn and the blood wept onto her neck.

Leadbeater ran into the courtyard, dressed now, and stopped aghast in front of Annie and Kali. She looked at him with unflinching eyes. Leadbeater quivered like a tethered horse in front of her, then backed away and ran back into the dark mansion. Annie stayed there, unmoving for some time, listening to the strains of a sitar in the far distance.

After all was quiet, she staggered back to her room and cleaned the cut. Blood could be washed away, but not this deeper wound of broken trust. She found herself sitting in the dark on a worn wooden chair as this horrible revelation crept into her consciousness.

So this is what betrayal feels like—this is what disillusionment feels like. She lit the oil lamp and would do what always comforted her, she would write. But this time there was nothing inspiring to share, nothing worthy of teaching, no informative or soothing word.

Charles Leadbeater was a—? She didn't even know if there was a word that describes a man who touches young boys this way. No one had ever talked to her about this; she would never have suspected this of such a noble man.

There certainly was only one solution, she thought. Charles must leave and she would have to be the one to send him away. Yes, she would see to it tomorrow morning. The thought of facing him again made her knuckles tighten around the chair. She felt as if she had lost her once-trusted and only friend.

And what to do with Krishnaji? How to talk to him? She must have that conversation with him, but even imagining talking to him now made her cringe. She got up, undressed and crawled into bed. Oh, for some comfort! She buried herself under the covers and tied to meditate but her thoughts raced; tomorrow she would also need to make arrangements for them to go to England. She would find him the best tutors there, give him a bicycle, teach him to ride a horse, and feed him such wholesome foods that he would become strong again. She would make it better....she would work to heal the trust that had been broken. She would.... she could....sleep finally came, although fitfully, and she awoke unrested.

Seventeen

Choices for British Brahmins

The next morning, Annie walked by Charles's bedroom door slowly; it was open and completely vacant. She peered in and saw a letter stuck upright on the table. She couldn't resist walking over to read the note:

My dear Annie:

I beg your forgiveness. I know you do not, and cannot be expected to understand me, but I meant no harm by my actions. I'm truly sorry if you think I've hurt Krishnaji, but I don't believe I have, as this was a ritual done by many ancient teachers over the years. I can't expect you to understand my ways.

Nevertheless I hope you will continue to believe in Krishnaji as the One, and that my clairvoyant powers have been accurate. I am leaving to go to Australia to work for the Society there. Please say good-by to him for me; he is the purest being I've ever seen and I will dearly miss him. And you.

Charles

She folded the letter and stuck it in her pocket. Doubts overcame her: Was she wrong? Did she over-react? She didn't think so, but there were things she didn't understand. She wondered if that sexual practice was a common practice back in ancient Greek times—Charles said he had lived then, but still, even if it was a left-over habit from one of his former lives—it was wrong.

He had done the right thing by leaving. But it didn't make sense how a man who could write such compassionate books as "*For Those Who Grieve*" and who had such knowledge of the chakras and clairvoyance, could allow himself.....no, she couldn't make sense of it.

Annie could see Nitya and Krishnaji playing cards outside the wall of the courtyard.

She walked over to them and asked Krishnaji to come with her. They walked back to the walled-in garden and sat again by the little pool. She wondered if he had seen her here last night.

"You look so serious, Amma." Krishnaji said.

"I need to talk to you about last night."

He spoke softly. "You don't have to come and explain, Nitya has told me about such things. I understand." He spoke softly and looked down. "And, last night, when I went back to the Masters, they said it was something Charles must do, but…I understand...you worry."

"You went back to the Masters last night?" Annie grit her teeth.

"Yes. Charles came and got me, and we finished writing this little book last night." He handed me the notebook *At the Feet of the Master* that he had shown me before. He said I should give it to you, and you would know what to do with it."

Annie took it. "I will keep it for you till you're older. It's a very wise little book from what I read so far, Krishnaji and I will keep it for you."

She paused. "But was Charles—was he doing the same thing…with you?" She braced herself.

"No, no—we just went to listen to the Masters, to pray and write what we learned." It was good that Krishnaji was calm and understanding it all this way.

"I'm so sorry for what he did…really, do you understand that? It wasn't right." He nodded his head. "And do you understand what is happening? What we're asking of you? I mean, do you think—do you feel—that you're the One?"

"How can I know?" He looked up straight into my eyes. "I like to be free to become whatever I'll become. I want to learn, to go to school, to make everyone happy."

He grinned. "And Amma, Nitya and I are excited to go to England and have adventures! We're ready."

And so it was to be. Krishnaji and Annie soon left for England where they would be taken in by her Theosophical friends there. She was going to care for the boys for some time, and would arrange for them to be taught by the finest tutors. She would soon have the boys bicycling, horse-back riding, studying, meditating, and happy again in no time.

There would also be doctor's visits to start, for both boys had bad coughs and she suspected lice as well. They had been living in poverty for years, with little medical attention, no mother and 5 other siblings. Annie was determined to do everything in her power to give them all the love and opportunities she could—they would be treated as British Brahmins. And she would spend years telling the world about the story of the boys and the coming of the new World Teacher.

What Annie didn't know then was that years later when the boy's father heard about Leadbeater's "inclinations" and the desire to create an *avatar* out of young Krishnamurti, he would bring Annie to trial to regain custody of the boys. However, he lost—despite his good objections. It was ultimately left up to the boys themselves if they wanted to stay with their father or Annie. They chose to stay with Annie.

Eighteen

Moments of Sacred Marigolds

When I think of Annie's life I often think of it as being divided into three parts: Annie as reformer and social activist in London, Annie's life after meeting Madame Blavatsky and adopting Krishnamurti, and Annie's life as passionate crusader and political force in India. The third part began happening in the years when Krishnamurti was at school in England and continued up until Annie's death in 1933. This chapter is the story of her love for India, and India's love for her.

What Annie did in India was a feat so spectacular that it alone would entitle her to a place in the pages of history. Many would say this was the time of her greatest achievement and personal victory.

As Gandhi once said: "There is no one in history who did more to inspire India for Home Rule than Annie Besant." She roused the Indians to feel pride in themselves and their rich spiritual history and opened the way for Gandhi to rise and come into the hearts of the Indian people.

Annie described Gandhi "as one of the earth's truly great men" and yet reminded her readers and listeners that she had first met Gandhi in 1889 at Madame Blavatsky's, and that it was Madame who gave him a copy of India's great spiritual book: the Bhagavad-Gita, reigniting his spirituality at a time when British law was his main preoccupation.

The Theosophical movement had been a shining light in India —it had done much for Indian self-confidence as it had treated the color and caste system with contempt and worked against child-marriage. And through the years, Annie was a tireless worker: she established the Indian Boy Scouts, schools for girls, and founded the Central Hindu College.

In 1894 when Annie was 47 years old she made India her second home; she bought a little bungalow and named it: *Shanti Kunja*: House of Peace. When in India, she wore sandals and a sari, and it was in India she returned to die in 1933.

In 1913, India was without home rule—one could say they were "homeless" in the sense that the country was divided into quarreling kingdoms and the British were the ones in power. The Indians were treated as second class citizens and Annie was outraged at the way the missionaries and the British business interests had crippled the Indians self-respect and self-confidence.

Annie was well aware that Theosophy had "borrowed" Hindu ideas of non-violence, karma, and reincarnation and Annie loved reminding the people of their rich spiritual legacy, though she was shocked to see the poverty and conditions for women and children. Forty years ago she had fought for rights and reforms in London, and now her life was being book-ended by similar passionate work. This time however, Annie had strong spiritual beliefs that 'held her' in a way she didn't have earlier. She had also proven her abilities as a lecturer and writer, and she was financially secure.

Annie's work started with a series of lectures with the title of "Wake-Up India" where she demanded an end to the petty animosities within India, the reform of child-marriage and the caste system, better rights for Indian women, and a revival of the *Panchayat*, the self-governing village council. To spread her message she started a weekly journal called the "*Commonwealth: A Journal of National Reform*" and it proved to be very popular and effective.

The Indians were astonished and flattered that this rather famous and upper class English woman would find them so worthy of her attention. She was the first British person to truly implant in them the seeds of self-respect; and they treated her like a spiritual mother wherever she went.

At that time, India had no national government, and was being run by raja kings, but it did have a National Congress that met once a year. This Congress was an important national symbol, however it was divided between moderates and extremists and didn't haven't much power. Annie was soon to change that.

So when Annie first became involved in India she did what she'd always done before—she bought and created newspapers. The first paper she bought was an old daily newspaper and reissued it as the *New India,* writing most of the editorials and regular columns herself. She imported a British cartoonist and a couple of writers to help her—the rest were all Indian. And—she traveled from one end of country to the other—speaking, campaigning and handing out newspapers and leaflets in an effort to arouse the Indian's dormant pride in themselves, their culture and their spiritual history.

Annie's newspaper stood for self-government and end to racial prejudice and better living conditions for the poor. Within a few months the paper had doubled its circulation. She was not demanding independent statehood for India, but self-government under

Britain—one would think of that as a moderate stance, but it wasn't at that time.

The Indians loved her, but many Theosophists and the British felt she was going too far—in fact the British distaste for her grew increasingly intense as she grew more and more popular. By the time she set up and organized the *Home Rule League* she was seen as a serious annoyance to the British.

They were actively hostile to her campaigning for home rule—which was just what she was doing—tirelessly traveling and speaking all over India. Annie was always happiest when she was working for the underdog, and she made a huge impact—so much so that when the Indian National Congress decided to adopt the doctrine of Home Rule as their own, they wanted her as the future President.

At this point the British had had enough! The police began following her, her mail was interfered with, her books were tabooed, and the British threatened to close the *New India.* But more than that, they felt she had to be stopped; but they didn't know what to do with her! They couldn't put this respectable English woman in jail, so they did the equivalent of that—they had her "interned" in a mountainous village, Ootacamund, where she could not leave, nor could she continue her publishing and speaking from there. They cut her off as much as they possibly could; even her mail was curtailed.

Ironically, one of the few pieces of mail that did get to Annie—and amused her greatly—was sent to her from Mr. George Bernard Shaw and was an essay he wrote called: "An Intelligent Woman's Guide to Socialism." Annie must have found that curious; perhaps wondering if he considered her an intelligent woman or not? At least he had signed the book "from a dear and old friend."

The truth was that Annie almost died there. If you remember, *work* was Annie's drug of choice, and she was now withdrawn from it. Now at this point in her life, she was nearing the age of seventy, and one would think she would have accepted this as a meditative retreat, but her heart wasn't in it. She had seen too much suffering, pain and injustice in India for her to relax. Unable to work, she became ill and withered instead.

Gandhi was called to help. He suggested a pilgrimage of volunteers to walk the thousand miles between Bombay and Ootacamund to arouse public concern, but the idea was turned down because of its 'impracticality.'

Eventually it was Annie's Theosophical friends in England who managed to press for her release, and after ninety-four days of internment, weak and ill, she was freed—and Indians everywhere were overjoyed. The British were not.

Her popularity was at its height now. On her return, the train stopped at every crossroad for the presentation of flowery garlands, wreaths and sandalwood from the peasants. The Brahmins brought her holy water from their temples. When she stepped out of the train at the Madras station her carriage was blanketed with flowers. The entire city of Madras was at the train station to meet her, and thousands of Indians lined the route from there to her home in Adyar. Once more filled with excitement for her mission, Annie began speaking again.

So in the winter of 1917, at the age of seventy, Annie became President of the Indian

National Congress. It was an unprecedented honor for Indian men, brought up under Eastern traditions to acclaim a woman, Annie Besant, as their president—the highest office in India. At that time, Indian middle class women lived and stayed in the home, had almost no rights, and if allowed outside the home were heavily veiled and guarded. However, Annie was treated as an incarnation of a deity.

It was quite a day—it was the largest Congress held so far, with some 9,000 people in attendance. There were banners and garlands, and bands playing, and it was said that the yellow glow of India's sacred marigolds was everywhere. Annie was dressed in a white sari, barefoot, wearing crystal beads and Helena Blavatsky's sacred ring. Her white hair gave her a numinous aura, and standing alone on the high rostrum it was said that she spoke with ease. Standing very still, hardly making a gesture, she had the radiance of a woman whose love was appreciated—her mellow voice swelling through the great tent as she spoke, her audience slipping under the enchantment of her spell.

However, it was not to last. After the grand ceremony, life and politics continued as usual. Always wanting to keep the peace, Annie tried to ease increasing tensions, but she was not quick to act in strong defense of the Indians when the long awaited reforms from the British were not forth coming and disappointing when they did come.

Meanwhile Gandhi was coming more into the public eye, speaking and arousing the minds and hearts of the Indians to pursue complete independence and to do it non-violently. He had found passive resistance the only possible weapon and an effective one in South Africa. And, he was one of them, an Indian man, deeply imbued with spiritual charisma.

He and Annie argued and disagreed about the best way to keep the peace and become independent, and then in April of 1919 Annie's attempts at moderate change and reform became undone. At Amritsar, in Punjab, the British General Dyer opened fired without warning on an unarmed gathering of Indians, killing 500 and wounding 1200 more. It was a defining moment in Indian history.

Annie was stunned, outraged, and for once didn't know what to do. She quickly struggled to get a constitution for a British-Indian commonwealth passed, but it didn't succeed. She was devastated at what the British had done, but could not resist reminding the public that she had predicted all along that Gandhian non-violence would lead to violence.

To this day, many historians still believe that if the Congress had followed her leadership, instead of following Gandhi, India would have been free and autonomous 17 years earlier and thus averted the split between Hindus and Muslims and the separation of Pakistan.

But at the time, the public didn't want to hear her brand of moderation anymore; she was an elder white woman whom they began discarding like a friend who had overstayed her welcome. They gave her an honorary doctorate in 1921, erected a statue in her memory, but kept their eyes on Gandhi. Particularly for the British, Annie Besant's name was finally being erased from history.

Nineteen

Ojai, California 1929

It was dusk. Annie was sitting at a baby grand piano playing Chopin's "Nocturne in E Flat Major" feeling its haunting mood. It was good to be in this little cottage in Ojai; in sunny California, and to know that Krishnaji and Nitya would be coming to stay here later today.

Nitya, who was now twenty-four, was coming on doctor's orders to cure his weak lungs and excruciating coughs brought on by living in chilly England. Annie had rented this cottage where they would all stay because the climate was said to be healing. It would be a chance for them to be together again after a long time spent apart.

Suddenly Annie felt a presence in the room. She turned around and looked into the shadows of the darkened room —there he was standing in the shadows! He had been listening to her without making a sound.

"Amma, I didn't know you played so well!" Krishnaji's voice shocked her. Annie gasped—this boy was no longer a boy, but a young man. Tall and thin, his dark suit and white shirt set off his classic features; high cheekbones, a long straight nose, full lips and sensitive dark eyes. His thick black hair was swept back. He walked out of the shadows towards her.

"Krishnaji! You're early!" She ran to hug the boy she hadn't seen for several years now. His schooling in England and her traveling kept separating them, though they wrote to each other weekly. Usually they'd be together several times a year for extended visits, but it had changed as he grew older.

"How are you? How you've changed!" The embrace was long and sweet. She barely knew what to say, but then it was obvious: "Where's Nitya?"

"He'll be here later. I took him to the doctors first."

"Good. But how did you get here so quickly?" She stood up.

He touched her cheek gently with his hand, and then slowly led her by the hand outside: "Come see. Isn't she a beauty?" There was a new car in the driveway; a convertible no less.

"But who gave you this? Gifts have expectations attached!"

"One of the Theosophists—you know how they are—you know how they love to give gifts, and I accept!" He beamed, but there was sarcasm in his voice.

"But there are expectations! You know that! It's not just the gifts but the Theosophists—well, you know what I mean." Her voice trailed off.

"I know about the 'gathering' or whatever you and Charles call it--he writes me all about it, and I don't like it! I don't feel up to it." He took out a letter from his pocket and thrust it at Annie. "Read it!"

In a whisper she read it aloud:

Dear Krishnaji,

I understand the final dates have been set for August 3rd and 4th at Castle Eerde in Holland for the Gathering ---for the 'Star of the East! One of our members has given you a castle! We are all so grateful. All of us here in Australia and those in Europe are eagerly awaiting the Second Coming. The moment of Truth is now upon us! Do you know that there are now over 43,000 members in 13 different countries? These are truly remarkable times. I look forward to seeing you soon. Fondly, Charles"

"They've given me a *castle*, Amma! Expectations? I…I can't do this!" His voice faltered. "I don't feel up for this—I know I agreed, but….why me?" He hit his hand against the wall letting it resound through the cottage till there was no sound. Annie stood frozen. "Why me?" He whispered and sank his head.

"What are you talking about? This is nothing new, not really…what's changed, Krishnaji?" Her eyes pleaded with him but she didn't want to know the answer. She turned away from him, tears filling her eyes.

"I've changed! But you—you and Charles—have been telling the world quite a story about me and you don't have any idea who I am!" Krishnaji had a hint of a smile on his face: "Sometimes I think it would be nice to go someplace where nobody knows my name and—play golf!"

"Golf?" Annie shook her head, running her hand through her hair.

"Yes, I've actually become very good at it in England."

"Krishnaji this is your chance to be whatever you can be—to tell us—whoever you are! And I'm here to give you that chance!"

"Amma! Half the world is expecting me to show up as some sort of Messiah, and…it gives me headaches. Honestly! I don't know what's going on. Perhaps I need a rest as much as Nitya."

They both sighed, obviously upset.

"You've mentioned your headaches in your letters. What's that about?" she asked.

He didn't say anything, so Annie slipped her arm through his and led him around the cottage to see the sun setting over the mountains.

"Ah, you see all that out there?" he said, pointing to the Topa Topa mountains. "It doesn't matter what any person says you are or aren't, but simply that you experience the fullness of it all; the mountain, the fresh air, the orange blossoms." His eyes became soft.

"You talk like a mystic...do you think you're a mystic?" Annie asked.

"I don't know, Amma, and I'd rather not talk about it." Annie looked down and said nothing as they walked back inside. She sat down at the piano again and began playing the piece she was playing when he walked in. The poignancy of the piece seemed to fit the mood.

She stopped. "I think you're a mystic! And I still believe Madame's prophecy will come true in some way—I don't understand it, but I believe, I'm sorry— I believe you will be a great teacher, whether you know it now or not!" She paused. "For me, Theosophy has been my path up the mountain."

His face changed, hardened. "Truth doesn't have a path! There are no ways! And, honestly, I don't understand Theosophy; the books, the initiations and rituals... Amma, I won't be put in a cage for anyone's worship!"

"I'm not asking you to do anything other than to speak your Truth! Whatever it is! Do you know who you are...I mean, do you have a sense that *someone has come through you* yet?

"No."

"No?

"No! No one, no Maitreya or Buddha or Jesus or Master." Krishnaji rubbed his head and ran his hand across the back of his neck.

"Amma—all your causes and grand passions and theories, can't you see? You're covering up your fear of being empty. Empty...that's what I am! *And hopefully free.*"

Krishnaji picked an orange blossom from a little cobalt vase on the piano and brought it to Annie. "Look." His voice softened. "How incredibly beautiful! When there is love inside you don't have to look for something to fill you from the outside."

"Are you in love?"

"No! Not in that way. But I have moments when I look into the emptiness—when I am totally present in the moment—I see that it is full."

"Full?"

"Full. And when you can do that, you will be free. It's quite a feeling." His face lit up.

"I don't know this emptiness you talk about…this being in the moment that way. What I want to know is when will you have the courage to speak—like that—to others? You're so quiet when other people are around. You seldom say things like that."

Silence.

Annie walked to the kitchen and motioned him to follow. "You must be hungry. Yes?"

"No. I'm fine."

Annie stopped and took his hand. "I love you. I simply want to know when you will speak your truth, no matter what it is? Everywhere you go people say you don't speak, or you say one thing that makes them think you are coming into your role as teacher, and another time you say nothing. Maybe this gathering is the time…"

He didn't reply. Instead he simply turned around and walked out the door.

Annie stood there. She had never seen this side of him before. A wave of disillusionment swept over her as she ran to the door again, opened it and waved good-by. He didn't turn back, and the mountains were barely visible—and yes, she could feel the emptiness, but it wasn't full.

Twenty

Breakdown

The next day Annie and Krishnaji drove into town to pick up some medicine for Nitya and get some groceries. By the time they got back to the cottage, she was more worried about Krishnaji than Nitya.

He started walking back and forth without saying a word, and rubbing the back of his neck. "What's wrong, Krishnaji?" she pleaded.

"The pain! This pain—it's in my neck and along my spine." He squirmed.

"Why don't you go outside and rest, lay down, while I make dinner?" Annie suggested. "Roselind will be over soon and you all can talk on the verandah."

He shrugged. "I'm going for a walk. I'll be back soon."

Roselind, a lovely young woman who Annie had hired to help care for Nitya, came over just as Krishnaji returned. The two of them were sitting outside on the verendah.

He seemed radiant. "Everything is so sparkling and green," Krishnaji exclaimed, "the green of England is nothing to this!" Ojai had been parched from lack of rain, and last night the first rains had come. He seemed enraptured by the beauty of what he had seen on his walk. He talked about the beauty of the orange groves, the setting sun over the mountains, the birds—it was almost too much.

He couldn't eat dinner, and things started changing as Krisnaji's mood plummeted from high to low. Nitya was tired and so went to his room, but Krishaji's eyes started glazing over. He started complaining about the heat, about the noise of the rattling window and the sound of a far-off plough. He complained that they were all 'full of nerves' and how it bothered him, and then went over and sat down on the floor in a dark corner of the room. They began hearing moans. They could see him trembling and shivering, clenching his teeth and hands.

"I don't know where I am! I want to go to India! Why have I been brought here?" He yelled, looking confused. Then suddenly the whole house seemed full of a terrific force and it was as if he was possessed. "I want to go to the woods!" he groaned. Then he was sobbing aloud, and no one dared touch him. He stayed in that dark corner of the room, still sobbing aloud that he wanted to go into the woods in India.

Rosalind went over to him, and put a wet cloth on his head, but then the moans became calls—"Amma! Where are you?" he called out, while rolling from side to side.

Annie crouched down next to him and gently lifted his head, nestling his head into her lap and started stroking his head. Rosalind held his feet as if to ground him. "Maybe we should get a doctor?" Annie suggested.

"No!" he screamed. "No doctor! Then he curled up in a fetal position and yelled at them not to touch him, and then later he'd call them back, crying like a child. He couldn't rest and couldn't be comforted. This went on for a couple of hours, and it was clear he was getting more and more exhausted. Suddenly he fell asleep and they covered him with a light blanket.

"Could this be a Kundalini-rising experience?" Rosalind whispered.

"I've never seen anything like this," Annie said, "but who knows? Madame called the backbone the path of the Serpent Fire—she and Charles used to talk about how this kundalini fire is strong enough to enlighten or... to cause psychosis."

"He's under a lot of pressure," Roselind added, "Do you think it's that? So much is expected of him…so soon. Maybe he doesn't feel up to it."

Annie shook her head. " I'll ask Nitya's doctor tomorrow….and I'll write to Charles about this, he might know if it's a kundalini breakthrough."

"You'd be wise to do that." Roselind gave Annie a weak smile. Everyone was completely unnerved.

Annie wrote to Charles: "The next night it was a variation of what went on the night before. He complains of a throbbing and burning at the nape of his neck and at the base of his spine. He can't stand noise. At times he wants quiet, and for no one to touch him. At other times he wants us to cradle his head and nurture him like a child. His moods vary by the hour. Charles, what is this?" She knew his answer would never arrive by post in time.

And again, the next day, the "process" began right after dinner. And every evening for about a week, some version of the process went on. He couldn't eat, and sleep only came in short intervals from exhaustion. They were all confused and worn down. The doctor had no idea what was happening.

On this one night, Rosalind, Krishnaji and Annie were sitting outside on the verandah when Annie saw that pained look come across his face again. But this time she had an idea.

She pointed to a huge tree in the yard. "Why don't you go sit outside under the Pepper tree, over there—?" He protested at first, but they could see he was already in pain and willing to do anything. Roselind gave him a blanket to sit on, and led him outside to the tree.

And so he sat there. It was a dark but starlit night, and the delicate hanging leaves of the tree were heavy with scented blossoms. They could see him sitting there, and hear him murmuring painfully. Suddenly there was silence. Then came a sigh of relief and he called out: "Oh, why didn't you send me out here before?" Then came another silence, and he began to chant. His voice was weary but steady, and he was still chanting by the time everyone went to their rooms for the night.

Annie kept peering out her bedroom window and she could see his face change from serene to agitated and then serene again. At times he rocked back and forth, and then he'd sigh and let out a moan. She was tempted to run out to him, and hold him again, but she didn't. Eventually, after checking with him one last time, he looked calm, and she fell asleep exhausted.

When they awoke in the morning he was still there. Totally quiet and unmoving. They decided to let him remain there unless he yelled out. Finally Annie could stand it no longer, and ran out to him. She was shocked by the altered presence that greeted her.

He began talking in a voice she never heard before: "There was a man mending the road; that man was myself; the pickax he held was myself; the very stone which he was breaking up was a part of me; the tender blade of grass was my very being, and the tree beside the man was myself. I almost could feel and think like the road-mender, and I could feel the wind passing through the tree, and the little ant on the blade of grass I could feel! The birds, the dust, and the very noise were a part of me. I was in everything, or rather everything was in me, the mountain, the worm, and all the breathing things."

His face was glowing, though his eyes were still glazed. He had lost so much weight he looked like a different person. Annie didn't know what to say.

"Amma—until I was able to say with certainty that I was one with the Beloved, I never spoke. I talked of vague generalities which I felt everyone wanted to hear. Now, all has changed. Can you understand?"

Annie hugged him—her lips trembling trying not to cry—and whispered, "You've found your voice...you've found yourself." It was as if he became another person overnight, and to Annie, he looked to be as enlightened a Being as she could imagine.

Twenty One

Roselind's Story 1988

The newspaper reporter who did the article on the screenplay writer, *Elizabeth Spring*—the one who was writing on the life of Annie Besant and Krishnamurti—quoted something *very wrong*, according to a woman who said she knew Krishnamurti *very well.* Her name was Roselind and she lived in the upper Ojai.

And so, I got a phone call to come over for tea as soon as possible to talk about this grievous error.

The light was already beginning to fail as I drove up the windy mountain road to Rosalind's house. She'd asked me to come for tea at four; a time when I'd usually be thinking about dinner plans and a large glass of cabernet sauvignon. She shared a house with the potter, Beatrice Wood, but she confided that Beatrice was away, and only Rosalind's old dog was there, and dying. She hoped I would understand if there were interruptions.

Rosalind was in her nineties then, and I was in my forties. I was a New Englander, and Rosalind had lived in California most of her life. Time and distance had separated us but I was thrilled to bridge this gap. Rosalind was well known for her connection to Krishnamurti.

She led me into her living room and motioned me to sit on her sofa. Her large old dog would be resting on a blanket between us. I carefully sat myself down on one side, and looked at what lay between us. There was love there, and tiredness, and the feeling of the ending of things. There was nothing to fear here with this dear creature, but Rosalind made me nervous. I could feel my face flushing, so I distracted myself by staring out a large window to the rolling hills beyond—hills on the land that Annie Besant had bought so many years ago.

Rosalind poured the tea and handed me a cup. She had called me to tea for one purpose, which she had briefly mentioned on the phone. She wanted to correct my grievous error concerning George Bernard Shaw and Annie Besant.

"They did not have an affair, they were not lovers!" she exclaimed. Her voice was proper, precise and uncompromising. I had shamelessly told the newspaper reporter who had come to interview me on my screenplay that they had an 'affair.'

Rosalind went on: "Annie may have loved him, but in those days, 'affairs' were not what a woman of integrity would do—and if nothing else, Annie was a woman of integrity." Rosalind sounded as if she was gearing up for verbal battle and I could feel a veil of mistrust drop down between us.

I began defending myself: "What they had between them may have been 'an affair of the heart.' Perhaps I was wrong to use that word because of the connotations." I pleaded. "Rosalind, you know between 1885 and 1887 they were *very close*—at times she supported him financially, they wrote poems to each other, they even played piano duets for their friends in the Socialist Party at that time…you must know this."

"That may be so, but still…." Rosalind stroked the dog's lean body and sighed. "People can be so harsh, and Annie was such a loving person."

I nodded my head. "I love Annie too. You know Annie's husband refused to give her a divorce, so Annie drew up a marriage contract for her and Shaw, as she hoped it would legalize their union. But Shaw didn't sign it—he was a bit of a slippery fish!"

Rosalind laughed and I dared to place my hand on the dogs back as well. I looked up at Rosalind. "Here we are talking about love, and assuming we know what their love was like, and assuming that negative judgments will be made—I don't think so."

Rosalind's eyes were glistening and her face looked weepy. Was it the dog? Or something else? "People who barely know me, judge me," she whispered. She wiped her eyes and turned away.

"Really?" That was hard to believe, but it looked as if she believed this was true.

"People knew that I was married to Krishnamurti's manager and....and that Krishnamurti and I were also a couple. What they didn't know is that my husband and I were completely estranged—he didn't want to have a marriage with me after our daughter was born. He ignored me, but stayed in the house....and during the war years the three of us began living together. It was Krishnaji who was more of a *husband* to me and a father to our daughter."

"Wow! Well, I don't judge you for that. There's a whole lot more story there, I'm sure." I took another sip of tea. We were from two different generations and it was easy for me not to judge.

Rosalind smiled at me and dabbed her eyes with a napkin. "Yes. My husband was older, an Indian, and in their culture men sometimes do that later in life."

I looked out her huge window wondering if I could see where the potter, Beatrice Wood had her studio, but all I saw were rolling green hills. I looked back at Roselind and her dog. "I love dogs; it must be hard for you to see him like this."

She nodded her head and smiled weakly. She looked frail herself, and spoke with a soft voice: "There's more that I want to tell you. I want you to know the Truth. For one; in the early days, before my marriage, I was deeply in love with Krishnaji's brother, Nitya, who died here in Ojai while Krishnaji was away. And something happened—I must tell you because it brought both of us out of our grief."

I sipped my tea and wished that I had a recording device with me. But I couldn't have been more open; I quivered with receptivity and listened to every word.

And so she began: "Krishnaji was in his twenties when he went with me and Annie and others to go on a ship heading to India. He left Nitya behind in Ojai because he believed what the Theosophists had said: that although Nitya was sick, he would not die when he was gone; that the Masters had told them that.

But when we were mid-route we received a telegram saying that Nitya was very ill, and a couple of hours later another telegram arrived saying that he had died.

Roselind looked at me realizing that she was sharing even more than she expected. "At first Krishnaji simply couldn't believe it. Krishnaji was never the same after that; he lost faith in Theosophy and the sadness was overwhelming, except for one thing, that softened it all. Perhaps it is what gave him his courage to speak later in life."

The dog lifted his head and nudged into my side.

And so she began: "The night that Nitya died I had a dream. I saw Nitya with a white silk scarf around his neck and I could tell in the dream that he was dying. He seemed in good spirits though and was happy to talk—he told me that I must remember meeting with him this night. But I said I was a bit of a 'doubting Thomas' and how could I be sure when I woke up that it was not just a dream?"

"Remember this scarf," he told me. "Remember to ask about a white scarf."

I asked him why he had the scarf around his neck and he said his throat was sore, and that I should ask a woman, a Mme de Manziarly, who cared for him that night, about this. And so I did just that. I asked her about that night and she said that she took off the white silk scarf that she was wearing and put it around Nitya's neck that night.

I paused and thought about that: "Ah… so it was proof that Nitya had come to you in the dream from the other-side, and that there was…and is, an afterlife."

"Yes." It was a comfort to both of us. "Nitya was a very pure Soul. Krishnamurti was a wise Soul, but it was almost as if he had two sides to him, and one side sometimes didn't know what the other was doing: the Teacher and the Man. Perhaps I was wrong to fall in love with Krishnaji later, but I did." The dog moaned.

"When Krishnaji was ill in Ojai—when he had days of what they called 'a painful and mysterious spiritual experience' I was there to comfort him. We were a couple for twenty-five years after those first few days in the cottage. It was not an affair, but really more of a marriage. Yet, in the last years of his life, even we drifted apart…" She stopped.

I looked into the dog's big brown eyes. "We're all so human, even when some of us are very wise." I added. "And does it really matter about Annie Besant? If she and Shaw loved each other, the rest is none of our business." Rosalind nodded in agreement.

The affection in the room had changed; Rosalind, the dog, and I were sitting there feeling the miracle of the story about the scarf, and the sweetness of this moment. The affection between the three of us was palpable.

I can't remember much more of the afternoon, but by the time I left it was dark, and my heart was light. I knew that there were deep connections and synchronistic moments, such as the dream and the scarf, that couldn't be explained away by common sense. Roselind had validated this for me. Sweet synchronicities happen to us all.

Twenty Two

At the Castle 1929

By the next week Krishnaji's "process" had calmed down enough so that they were able to take off for the convention at Castle Eerde in Holland. Krishnaji agreed to go with no protest.

This castle was the place of the long awaited gathering, the place where 3,000 Theosophists were expected to gather to hear Krishnamurti accept his role as world teacher.

When they arrived a swarm of journalists and curious people surrounded them. One journalist yelled out: "Mrs. Besant—is he the new Messiah you've proclaimed?"

Annie was ruffled by his outburst. "As I've carefully explained before, and I'll do so again—is that Krishnamurti..." Another journalist burst in: "Is this the man you're calling the next Messiah? Is he the Christ? This 'Krish-neri'?"

Annie looked over at Krishnaji: "He can speak for himself. And you can call him K."

K turned and looked at the man. The crowd became silent. "Don't be concerned with the vessel that may or may not contain Truth; drink of the water yourself—yes?"

K smiled serenely at the reporter, and they retreated inside the cool manor house. They were greeted immediately by Colonel Olcott, who had apparently just arrived from India with another man.

Olcott introduced K to Mr. Fenstermacher: " This is the young man I've been telling you about."

"So pleased to meet you!" I've heard so much about you, from Col. Olcott here." They shook hands and looked at each other speechless for a moment. Then Mr. Fenstermacher whispered into his ear: "So, forgive me for being so bold, but in light of everything, does it matter that Oxford didn't accept you?" He hadn't whispered it softly; everyone heard.

"No. I didn't pass the exam." K looked totally unmoved.

Mr. Fenstermacher coughed, then realizing his rudeness tried to change the subject: "Of course, you're involved with spiritual studies, yes? You know many people say there are significant parallels between the teaching of Buddha and those of Jesus—would you agree?"

"I don't know. I don't like comparisons." K stood absolutely still like an animal caught, defenseless and unmovable.

"Ah, you're the more contemplative type, I can see." Mr. Fenstermacher smiled.

Olcott must have felt a need to step into the conversation now, but whether it was to defend or accuse, Annie couldn't tell. "India has a history of contemplatives…but you, Krishnamurti, would you say you're the new proto-type of Blavatsky's 6th root race?"

"What?"

"You know, from *The Secret Doctrine*: the 6th sub-race." Olcott elaborated.

"I haven't read it."

"Never read it? So what do you do then?" Olcott looked anything but pleased.

"I work on my car. I'm a scratch golfer. I read....and walk. I like being outside."

Olcott slapped him on the back laughing. "Hah! Leave the esoteric stuff to us old-timers, eh?" He then led them into another room where there was an even larger group awaiting. He raised his arms and quieted the crowd.

"Can I have your attention, please! We're so very fortunate to have young Krishnamurti with us today, and since we're all so full of questions for him, why don't we begin?"

He led K up to a podium next to an enormous window with a view of the rolling hills and mountains.

A woman spoke up first. "Tell us please, what is it you really desire to do?"

He looked down and said nothing. Annie felt sick. Then he pointed out the window—

"You see all that out there? I have the desire to enter into that."

Everyone turned to look at the patterns of light and shadow moving across the lawns.

"I know my destiny and my work. I long to make everyone happy. What can I say? Life is a strange business. Happy is the man who is nothing; empty."

"Are you nothing; empty?" Mr. Fenstermacher asked.

"I'm trying to be."

"How many hours a day do you spend meditating?" A man asked.

"I don't. I try to stay consciously aware; awake; inquiring…."

A woman spoke out from the audience: "Krishnamurti, tell us now, are you enlightened?"

Silence.

"Tell us, are you the One whom this woman says you are?" She pointed at Annie.

K was beginning to look annoyed. "If you have an image of who I should be, then you can't see me, can you? If God himself were to show up here, could you recognize him? Tell me, could you?" Not a sound could be heard.

Then Annie saw him. It was Charles. He had written to Annie that nothing would stop him from being there, though he had to come all the way from Australia, where Annie had urged him to remain so many years ago. Although they wrote occasionally, she hadn't seen him in a long while. She knew he proclaimed the arrival of the new "Avatar" wherever he went.

Leadbeater must have felt the need to rescue his Theosophical protégé. Raising his voice he said: "Krishnaji is being prepared, by the Masters to accept the Soul of the One. We must be patient. We don't know when this will happen…now, enough! Let's give this good man and woman some rest!"

Then Olcott quickly took Krishnamurti away from the crowds and the madness. Annie looked around to find Charles.

He was standing in the back looking confused and annoyed. They shook hands formally. He whispered, or rather hissed: "It looks like "The Coming" is going wrong! And now is not the time to be wrong! If something is wrong, it's that you didn't raise him right—I saw what he could be; what he will be!"

Annie stepped back. She couldn't believe that a man who had written so many wise books and who had discovered Krishnaji, could be so vehement.

"He'll be who he will be, Charles. He's not going to be used by anyone!"

"He's going to be used—by God! Our God! This is a revolution in the world of the Spirit. Have you forgotten?"

"I've forgotten nothing! I have traveled the world too—trying to prepare people for the new message Krishnaji will give us. But do you ever think you may be deceiving yourself about your role in this?" she added.

"No…it's not just me, but *we* have been proclaiming Madame's message to the world. And there are thousands of people waiting for what he will say—this Saturday! Have you ever considered the money these people have poured into the Society because they believe in him? *In you? In us?* What is going to happen to you when you have nothing—when he's left you? You think they'll want you around after he's destroyed everything you've worked for? Talk some sense into him!"

"No. You're ranting, Charles."

He sneered at her. "There is nothing I cannot extinguish…as easily as crushing an egg in my hand, for the sake of a cause I believe in!"

"A cause? Krishnaji is not your cause; you're acting crazy."

"If you won't take care of things, I will. Where is he?" Charles said ruthlessly. Annie turned and walked away quickly.

Twenty Three

Rituals, Rites and Roses

It was said that Krishnamurti had disappeared—that he had gone off into the forest outside the Castle grounds to retreat. No one really knew where he was—Charles was infuriated.

That night Annie heard that Charles was inviting people to a ritual, a kind of 'high mass' in the chapel at the castle and it proved to be true.

Annie's curiosity got the best of her.

She stood in the back of the chapel in the shadows and watched. Charles was dressed in a purple satin robe with a huge gold cross around his neck. He looked like a priest, presiding over a dimly lit "mass" with a small group of people sitting around him. The room was lit by candlelight and the incense was thick.

And so he began: "We are gathered here today to prepare for the coming of the Avatar; the World Teacher. As was done in the past, and what will be done now, is the formation of a group of severs; of apostles, who will assist the World Teacher."

Charles arranged a few things on the altar, turned back, and began: "I have chosen each one of you carefully. Please come forward as I call your names: James Wedgewood, George Arundale, Rajagopal, Henry Olcott…." As if in a trance, each man went to the front as Charles droned on in English and Sanskrit.

He offered each of the men a lit candle, which they in turn, placed in a large Menorah-like candle holder. He lit the last candle for himself.

On a separate tall pedestal was one remaining candle. He took it down and raised it high saying: "This candle must remain unlit until tomorrow when He with his own Divine hand shall light it, and bring new guidance to our hearts and lives. Krishnamurti has unknowingly passed another initiation, and is now an adept of the highest rank. He has gone into the wilderness to pray today, and it is now up to us to pray for him."

He set the candleholder down and began strutting in front of the men; looking intently at his posse. Then he spotted Annie in the rear of the chapel. He walked back to the altar, and looked quickly for another candle, but spotting none, he took the one rose from the altar, and raised it high.

"This rose is the rose of our Divine Mother; Annie Besant. Please come forward."

Annie froze. Then she slowly walked down the aisle wondering what she would do, knowing she had to do something. Must she accept it? She was quivering. Then she remembered Kali, the negative mother, the one who would extinguish light.

"Take it," he whispered to her. "Take it!"

Annie took the rose in her hand, and panic struck. This wasn't right. This must be undone. With barely a thought, she took the large rose, bent the stem, and using it like a candle sniffer, extinguished each one of the flames that had been lit. Like she had once done so many years ago at Frank Besant's Church, she again walked down the aisle, and out of "Leadbeater's Church."

Twenty Four

"The Coming Has Gone Wrong"
August 3, 1929

It was about to begin. A few people were still gathering wood for campfires and many were setting up little "altars" with Krishnmurti's picture surrounded by candles. Annie walked among the campgrounds while it was still light and stopped at a little altar dedicated to Krishnaji.

A young boy was standing over a table selling candles. Many of the candles had been warped by the hot August sun.

He recognized her. "Mrs. Besant, would you like one?"

"What are you selling?" She asked, noticing the coin box.

"They're candles that have been blessed by Krishnamurti---Mr. Leadbeater said so."

"Mr. Leadbeater gave you these to sell?" Annie said through gritted teeth.

"For you they're free."

She bent down next to the boy, struck a match and lit a candle. She held it up to the sun. "Now look at the flame and look at the sun."

"They're the same fire aren't they?" he said.

"Exactly. You have the same fire in you. We all have the same flame in us that Krishnamurti has…just like this flame is the same as the sun. But I used to be like this candle." Annie pointed to a melted candle.

"Like that? Why?"

"When we don't know our own inner light we feel we need to be close to the sun all the time…but we can melt that way…become distorted. At times we're all like candles in the sun. We think we're the only ones who have the truth, the light, and we think it's our duty to light more lights and make more candles…but do you know what?"

He shook his head, not knowing what I would say.

"We become warped; useless. Who needs candles in the sun?"

"That's an interesting question, Mrs. Besant…" A different voice quivered next to Annie. She stood up. There was a young woman standing before her; a scarf draped over her head.

"Yes?"

"You don't recognize me, do you? It's been that long."

"No…"

"I've been trying to get up enough courage to talk to you, for the longest time."

"You don't need to be scared of me. Come sit." Annie patted the ground.

The girl took a deep breath. " haven't seen you for almost twenty years. You sent me letters, but Papa didn't approve of me writing to you so much."

Annie stared at her, seeing something of her face in the girl's face: "Mabel?! Mabel!

"Mother!" They hugged each other so long; they finally burst out laughing.

Annie held her at arm's length for a second to see her better. "I always hoped you would find me...and come to me again... someday."

"I've followed everything you did; I was so proud of you. But I stopped writing because I was so confused."

"I can understand that...and I was afraid your father had turned you against me."

"Well, I was mad at you for a few years there. I stopped writing because you'd become like a distant star to me. You don't know how you affect others; Shaw was the one who insisted I should come see you."

"Oh, Mabel...I don't know what to say. I've always missed you terribly. You've been my private sorrow."

Mabel's eyes were teary. Annie reached out her hand to her and they stood up. "We have a lot to catch up on" Annie said, "But let's go, together, because it's about to start."

They walked back through the crowds and up to the center stage. There was a huge campfire already lit, and Annie could see Leadbeater and his band of "apostles" in the front near the platform. Where was Krishnamurti?

Annie slowly rose to the stage, with Mabel next to her, and spoke:

"Many years ago a very wise woman had a dream—a vision of a great teacher who would lead us out of ignorance into Truth. She saw a New Age coming which would honor the perennial and mystic wisdom which is at the heart of all religions…" She paused and searched the crowd for Krishnaji.

"The dream, that Madame Blavatsky dreamed, is indeed here today with us. Is it not in each and every one of us? In this New Age? The message will be new." Annie scanned the crowd again—he wasn't there.

She looked at Mabel. She had to go on, but her voice was shaky and not as strong: "Once I listened with my head, not my heart, so I could not hear clearly. Now I try to listen with my heart and know that all people; lovers, friends, children, are my teachers in this New Age."

A heckler in the crowd yelled out: "Where's Krishnamurti?"

She saw him then. He had been standing in the back and she could see him coming forward now. He rose to the podium.

Krishnamurti looked out over the crowd and spoke softly. "I am here. But I must tell you that as soon as I began to think for myself, I found myself in revolt. It is now my purpose to spread that spirit of revolt which has led me to truth."

"Can't hear you!" Another heckler yelled out.

He cleared his throat and spoke loudly: "For years people have been worshipping a picture which had not spoken; now I am here! And I am here to tell you that I am not who you were hoping for—you can form other organizations and expect someone else. You can build other cages, but I will not be brought into a cage for your worship." He paused, and a murmur went the crowd.

"My only concern, the only thing I can teach you, is how to become absolutely unconditionally free. Can you hear that? I maintain that Truth is a pathless land, and you cannot approach it by any path whatsoever—Truth, being limitless, unconditioned, cannot be organized;

nor should any organization be formed to lead people along any particular path—I want you to be free from all fears—from the fear of religion, from the fear of death, from the fear of life itself. You can form other organizations, expect someone else, but my only concern is to set men absolutely, unconditionally free."

Krishnaji looked at Annie and stepped back. The crowds looked stunned. There was an awkward silence and then some weak applause, and a vague din—they didn't understand what he just said.

Annie squeezed Mabel's hand, and then rose to the podium again: "I have heard the message you just heard—don't listen to Krishnaji and say you understand. Listen to your heart, and know that there is no voice more worthy listening to than the one in here… as Madame Blavatsky once said: *'There is no religion higher than Truth.'* Now we must each find that Truth for ourselves."

When Annie stepped down, Leadbeater had disappeared. All she could hear were mutterings, shouts and weeping. Everywhere it was clear that: "The Coming had gone wrong."

And so this chapter of Annie's life closed, but never the love between Annie and Krishnamurti. After this, Annie returned to India, and continued to champion the cause of Home Rule for the Indians. Krishnaji was always to call her "Amma" and he would visit her in India up until her death.

Twenty Five

Christmas Eve, Ojai 1988

It was Christmas Eve. The "stockings were hung by the chimney with care" but visons of sugarplums didn't dance in her head. Mother would be arriving any minute; Harry and Sarah were picking her up at the Santa Barbara airport. I had been cooking and cleaning all day and was already tired on my feet. I looked at the thermometer—it was almost 90 degrees on this Christmas Eve; quite unlike a New England Christmas.

I suspected mother wouldn't be pleased with the heat but there were some things I couldn't change. Or could I? I turned on the air-conditioner—that would help! I'd already put fresh flowers in the guest room and turned on a little holiday music. There would be no "white Christmas" this year as I fondly remembered the Christmas' eves of my childhood. Weren't they all white?

It looked as if I'd have a few moments for myself before they arrived. So I mused; no, I worried. I needed to stop worrying about things that were not perfect enough and deadlines that needed to be met. The screenplay contest deadline of January 15th was looming close, and though I'd been working on the screenplay for a month now it was far from finished. I knew it was cutting it close to have mother here now, but there was no choice.

I was thinking of the Serenity prayer as I sat down next to the Christmas tree and picked up a book called "The Last Four Lives of Annie Besant" by Arthur Nethercot. It was a two volume set, full of detailed information. The first book was called "The First Five Lives of Annie Besant." What did he think she was—a cat with nine lives?

As I was finishing up the last chapter I saw it: the author was writing about Annie's Vasanta

Publishing Press in India, and explaining that the word "*Vasanta*" is a Sanskrit word meaning "*Spring*"—my last name—and that *Spring* was a word regarded in India as the equivalent of the name "*Besant.*" What?

I read it again. Did I understand this right? That's right: Vasanta = Spring = Besant. That's what he said… a shiver went through me. Besant and Spring; another little drop of sweet synchronicity. *Thank you Annie,* I said, closing the book. It felt like a Christmas present.

Just then they arrived.

"How was your trip?" I asked while hugging Mom, who was feeling more like an angry cat about to pounce, than a mother.

"Awful. Just awful. You wouldn't believe what I had to deal with, Janet—I just can't do this flying anymore. The lines! The traffic! And the heat here! My goodness, this doesn't feel like Christmas in this weather!"

"How come you still call Mom, Janet, instead of Elizabeth?" Sarah asked.

"Because that's what I named her!" she attempted a smile.

"Do you like the tree? I made some of the ornaments." Sarah took an ornament off the tree and handed it to her. "This is the gingerbread grandmother I made for you."

She looked at the ornament and nodded. "This is very nice, honey," she said, looking at Sarah, "but you wouldn't believe *how long* it took the taxi to pick me up this morning…I just can't do this again. Ever. Ever! I'm too old for this." She did the classic "swiping your hand across your forehead" move as Harry gave me his "look" that said he'd had just about enough of her.

Sarah walked over to the tree and put a candy cane in her mouth. "And Janet, you've got to stop letting Sarah have so much candy!" She turned and whispered to me, "*I love you, but you know this situation with the sugar is something— I care very much about—it's hurting her.*" I bit my tongue, and made a decision not to argue.

Instead I told them the discovery I had just made—the little synchronicity of the names Besant and Spring. Harry was astonished. I guess mother didn't really get why I was excited, as she just shrugged her shoulders. Sarah listened and kept licking the candy cane. I wondered what she was thinking; I was sure she was picking up on the edgy energy in the room but she just kept smiling.

After dropping off mother's bags in the guest room, we managed to have a pleasant Christmas Eve dinner and the presents were opened. Everyone was pleased. Mother had brought a few small gifts for each of us, and we had a few gifts for her that weren't too big for her to carry home. Then she asked us to wait while she went back to the guest room.

"For you," she said, returning to the living room, and handing me a package about the size of a large book. "It's not really all that good, but still, I wanted you to have something of mine." Suddenly, she looked shy; an unusual expression for her.

I tore off the wrapper and gazed at a lovely little oil painting of a single bird on a branch, singing into the night sky. "This is so beautiful, Mom! I love it! You did this!" I exclaimed while hugging her. I was truly surprised she had brought it all this way.

The rest of the evening went well, ending with kisses all around, and my fears were eased for the moment. Maybe things would be different this time!

~

After the next few days of showing Mom all the little shops in the Arcade, the parks and mountain views, Krotona, the health food store, and the various other 'spots' to see in Ojai, we settled into a routine: I would write from 7:00 am until noon, then we'd have the afternoons and early evenings together. I'd go back to writing after Sarah was in bed. This lasted for a couple of days.

Then Mother started complaining of not feeling well. "If you didn't have to work so much I might feel better," She declared. "I really don't understand why you find that other woman so interesting to write about."

What could I say? I tried a few explanations; nothing worked.

She would sit listless on the sofa most of the morning, and then in the afternoon she'd only want to sit outside in the shade. I would sit near her, but in the sun. At dinner she just picked at her food.

This was depression as far as I could tell, and I knew any suggestion on my part would be answered with a 'yes, but…' but I tried anyway. "Why don't you consider moving out here?" I suggested. "There are some retirement communities…."

"Janet, you know how much I love you, but when you left New England to come out here, it was just too much! I can't make a change like that." She had a horrible look on her face, and the guilt seeped into me. We talked more about her moving here, but then I gave up on that idea.

I suggested she see my doctor, as she was developing a cold. I was getting anxious as well; the screenplay was moving along very slowly and mother was winding down. The complaints had gone from full volume to a quiet despair, and a look of weariness veiled her face.

By the time I got her to my doctor, it was obvious what she had—anger and depression. But what was diagnosed, was a bad cold.

She thought she was dying. She went to bed and I begrudgingly played the good daughter, bringing her meals in her room and reading to her. My long hours of writing were gone. We sat together hour after hour, and if I did my writing it only aggravated her more. *Why had there always been so much difficulty between us? I felt our sorrow and yet felt the love beneath it all.*

It appeared that things couldn't get more depressing, till she announced that she couldn't eat anymore. I tried, I begged, I reasoned and I pleaded. *Perhaps she had decided that she was going to die with us—or simply never go back?*

But tonight when I brought her food it was different. She picked a little more at the food, then closed her eyes, and said no. I walked back into the kitchen and stood there dumbfounded. Then I saw the pumpkin pie I had made for dessert. She always loved pumpkin pie with ice cream.

I returned to her room with the pie and ice cream. "Mom, open your eyes." She barely stirred. "Come now, open your mouth…" I placed a little piece of pie and ice cream on the fork and put it up to her mouth. She opened and slowly swallowed. I picked up another piece and slowly fed her a second piece. And a third. She was like a child again, my sick child, and along with each mouthful a new sweetness filled the room. A little smile appeared. I kept feeding her. She smiled more.

When I finished she put her hand over mine. I looked down at our hands together—I hadn't ever noticed how old her hands looked, I hadn't ever really thought about seventy year old hands. They looked thin and fragile; the blue veins rising out of the skin like river-ways over a parched land. "I love you," I whispered, then stood up and pulled the blanket over her lightly, tucking her in. She looked up at me and repeated: "I love you too."

I waited for the usual refrain of "*I love you but.*" It didn't happen. I could count on the fingers of one hand the number of times in my life when "I love you" wasn't followed by a "but." I was shocked.

Things began getting better. The next day at her bedtime I brought out some old photograph albums and we looked over pictures of my childhood and was surprised by how much happiness I saw there and remembered.

"So, Janet, why do you think this woman you're writing about is so…special to you? I don't get it," she asked.

"I'm not sure." I said. "But you remember about the similar charts, don't you?"

"You don't really believe in that do you?" I looked away and didn't say anything. I had stopped hoping that she would believe in my astrological work years ago.

"Do you think she's like a mother to you?" she asked. "Someone better than I was?"

"No. We all just do the best we can do, right? I'm no saint." I laughed, but felt like I wanted to run away; or run towards something. A heat began building in my gut and coming up over me like a hot flash. It kept building, rising up from someplace deep inside. I broke out into a sweat.

It was the question. Who was Annie to me? I asked myself: What was my obsession with Annie? Unresolved mother issues or what? Was Annie "on the other side" wanting me to write her story? *Yes*. Was I once Annie? *Yes*. Yes? Where did that come from…. Yes!?

For a moment I felt dizzy from the force of the thoughts and the shock of the answer. I braced myself against her bed, and brought myself back to this reality. I adjusted her pillows and sank down on her bed. We were silent for a moment.

What would Annie do now? I wondered, as I began stroking her head like a sick child. "It's going to be alright, Mom, it really is going to all be alright... just get some rest now." I stayed a few minutes longer, stroking her head till she fell asleep, and finally got up and turned off the light.

And then I went back into my room and looked at my astrology chart. It was one thing to feel, to intuit, to hear something, but was it there in the chart? What hadn't I seen before?

My eyes circled the chart and lingered over my South Node. This would be the spot on my chart which would speak of my past life…and there it was in Scorpio in the 8th house conjuncting Jupiter. I knew that the South Node in Scorpio here, next to Jupiter, suggests a past life that was large (Jupiter) and dramatic (Scorpio)—filled with many chapters where the Soul was experiencing phoenix-like experiences of death/rebirth and regeneration as layers of the past were being stripped away. Scorpio yearns for the bottom line Truth and goes into what is hidden or taboo or occult to find itself. *Sounds like Annie.* I sighed…

What else? I scanned the astrology bookshelf and took out one book, searching through the pages till I heard what this author had to say about my configuration in the 8th house: "You were most likely the person 'behind the throne' in a former life; one who was in relationship with a powerful person who you influenced and yet who may have overshadowed you." *Annie was often overshadowed by Krishnamurti and Blavatsky.*

The more I read, the more accurate the description became…it went on to say that because there was a largeness and perhaps wealth or notoriety in my last life, the trauma of it all would make the Soul seek serenity in this life (my corresponding North Node in Taurus) and would find peace in finding the sacred in the commonplace. Hm…a simpler life. A family life? A life as a mother and wife, a potter and writer? A woman who was still looking beneath the surface of things for the real meanings… an astrologer? Why not?

I sat at my desk and gradually the heat in my body receded, and then the words flowed… it was then that I knew I had Annie's story in my bones.

By the time Mother was scheduled to leave, she had been hand fed, read to, and sat with for so long I think she'd had enough…she was ready to go back. When I took her to the airport, the last thing we said to each other was I love you, and there were no *"buts"* this time. I cried all the way home for the gifts we had each received.

However, it was now Jan 10th and the screenplay deadline was in 5 days. I wasn't finished and yet I wasn't anxious. I just worked; all day long every day, and on the 5th day I drove into Santa Barbara and handed in my screenplay along with all the others. There must have been close to fifty screenplays, and I knew now why I had to push myself so hard for this. My part was to tell Annie's story; that was my part of the collaboration—if more would happen, it would have to come from Annie.

Twenty Six

The Contest, the Option, and the Choice

"The 3rd Place Award goes to Christina Nickolson for her screenplay: *An Unchosen Life*." Christina looked like she was sitting with her parents, and she rose to the stage blushing as the crowd applauded. She smiled and quickly returned to her seat.

I squirmed in my chair. I was already disappointed. I was trying not to expect too much, but it could have made it to third place! Maybe Annie wasn't having any collaboration in this part of the process—after all, it was just a contest. But still, getting an award would have helped me get the screenplay into the right hands. I wished I hadn't asked Harry to come; it was just doubling the shame of my overly high expectations.

"The Second Place Award tonight goes to…Mark Olveti! This is for his screenplay *Malevolent Intentions*." Again the applause, as a young tattooed man leapt out of his chair and sauntered up to the stage. He acted like he was getting an academy award—his grin as wide as his face. He kept looking around, repeating thank you, thank you…and continued shaking the presenter's hand until the presenter pointed to the stairs for him to go down. He beamed, and I was happy for him.

"The First Place Award, this year, at the Santa Barbara Screenwriter's Guild goes to……" And then he paused, like they so often do to build the excitement. "You know the Guild has been giving these awards out for almost 20 years now and many of our winners have seen their screenplays go on to be produced. And it is indeed an honor to present this award, as it acknowledges the writer's efforts and excellence in writing. All of us here at the Guild feel very proud this year to offer the

Santa Barbara Screenwriters First Place award to a new member of the guild…..to… Elizabeth Spring, for her screenplay "*Sweet Synchronicity.*"

The tears rushed to my eyes—this was the last thing I wanted to happen at this moment, but there was no containing it. Harry hugged me, brushed away my tears and whispered in my ear: "Go up there honey, you did it!"

I stood up and made my way forward. *Don't trip, I thought to myself.* I rose to the platform as if in a dream. As I took the marble/quill pen award the presenter handed me, and added, in a very large voice: "So as our first prize winner, is there anything you'd like to say to our members and fellow writers?

I wasn't expecting that. But yes, of course—"I'd like to thank the Santa Barbara Screenwriter's Guild very much for this honor and to acknowledging the effort it took all of us to create these screenplays." I looked around at all the expectant faces, and wondered what I really wanted to say: "And I'd especially like to thank my husband Harry Spring, for all his support…. and I'd like to thank my muse, Annie Besant, for her help in this!" I closed my eyes for a second and imagined her accepting the award with me, and then, without thinking, I raised my hands in the air and loudly exclaimed—"We did it, Annie!"

They gave me a standing ovation—I guessed this must be the tradition for all first place winners, but being that it was my first time here, I was more than surprised! The tears began to flow again but my heart was bursting. Somehow I managed to stand there, taking in this delicious moment.

And suddenly it was over. Harry and I lingered in the rear of the hall to mingle with the members and judges. Some people left immediately.

"So would my famous writer-wife like a glass of wine?" Harry asked.

I nodded and watched him make his way to the wine table. At last I could begin to catch my breath again.

"You're Elizabeth? Congratulations!" An older dark-haired woman edged her way over to me. She held out her hand—"Katherine Kindley." She had the most "masculine handshake" I've ever felt.

The dark haired woman in the tailored suit lost no time in stating her intention: "I'd like to "option" your screenplay—I know quite a few people in the business, and, if you'd be willing, I'd like to do a 6 month option and am willing to pay $5000. How does that sound?"

I gasped. It sounded unreal. I knew that finding someone to "option" your work was how screenplays got around to producers and actors, but never expected anything like this ....not this quick, not just now.

She handed me her card. I noticed the Montecito address; she lived in the wealthiest neighborhood in Santa Barbara, and I suspected she did have connections.

"Can you come by tomorrow, say at eleven?" she asked, assuming the answer, and allowing her eyes to flit around the room. I'm never completely comfortable with people who don't make good eye contact.

"Of course. I'll be there." I replied. "Do I need to bring anything?"

"No, just the screenplay dear," she laughed. "I'll have the check ready."

And then she disappeared as fast as she came.

~

Neither she, nor the check, was ready the next morning at eleven when I arrived at her plush Montecito estate. I was ushered into a waiting room, and I did just that…I waited. I was hoping she'd appear soon, as I was getting so increasingly nervous. I kept thinking about the questions I hadn't ask her; like if we needed to have a lawyer, or how and when I'd get the screenplay back.

I waited. The parlor had a high ceiling, floor to ceiling windows, and a filigree gold and white fireplace. I didn't like the way the room felt; cold. I glanced at my watch. She had kept me waiting 15 minutes now. Was this usual?

Finally she walked in, apologizing for her lateness. She led me into another room that appeared to be her office. She sat at a desk, motioned me to sit, and took out her checkbook. "Spring, right?"

"Yes. But tell me, is this all we do now?" We don't need any contract, or lawyer?"

"No, but look here, I'll write this up: this guarantees that Katherine Kindley has a 6 month option on the screenplay "Sweet Synchronicity" to be returned no later than July 16th. OK?" She slid the paper across the desk.

It was then that I noticed she had several books on her desk—on Krishnamurti. The top one had just been published, but I had read it.What do you think of this one?" I asked, touching the cover of the new book. Her eyes lit up. "Amazing, isn't it!" This information will change everything! People thought this Krishnamurti was such a holy man—a celibate—now they'll see! He had a 'wife' for almost 25 years! This is going to have to be included in this screenplay. I know another writer who could do it—or if you wanted, he could help you with this."

"What?" I couldn't believe what she was telling me to do.

I started to stutter: "I know—I know—about that book, but that's not what this story is about! It's about two imperfect but amazing people—wise people."

"And one who did a very unwise thing as well!" She gave me a knowing smile.

So she was going to change the screenplay and make it into a cheap expose. I looked at the check made out to me for $5000, ripped it in half, and handed it back to her.

"No thank you, Ms. Kindley. You can find someone else to write it for you but that's not what this story is about."

She stood up quickly. "I'll do just that then. You're making a foolish decision, Ms. Spring—you're too idealistic for this business—your screenplay will never sell as it is. It has to have more "juice" to it! It needs this." She pointed to the book. "Sex sells."

I laughed. "Not with my name on it! Inspiration sells too; and finding out what's beneath the public facts. Did you even read the screenplay?"

"No, but my husband did; he was one of the judges. He said it was good. But he doesn't know what I know—he doesn't know about this book, here, and he doesn't know what sells."

With that, I took the screenplay out of her hands and left. I felt almost as good about refusing her as winning the award. *"Annie, take care of the rest," I said aloud as I jumped into my car. "It's your turn now!"* It would be Annie's turn now to find a way "to birth" this story into the world. And I believed she could do it; in some way, somehow.

Twenty Seven

End Notes: The Occultist, the Mystic, and the Astrologer

While writing this book I found that I needed to have a break in my writing every day, and it wasn't enough to just go for a walk or take time out for lunch. I wanted to take time to meditate; to lie down, put on my favorite incense and soothing music and do something that Carl Jung called "active imagination." This practice of using the mind imaginatively was also used by occultists, such as Annie and Charles, and it was called *kriyashakti.*

This technique of "thought power in action" is based on the theory that the mind has the power to create "thought forms" and it can then "see" the things that it has created. This visualizing power is the way images, dreams and revelations are built, and problems solved. Many people, including writers and scientists use this imaginative technique and can use it to find answers to questions.

A clairvoyant or an occultist practices it using it deliberately to be receptive to thought forms around them, or to create a thought-image and then observe it. Many musicians and artists, particularly modern abstract artists, use it naturally and unconsciously.

And, if there is a yearning and a longing in the heart to create or see something, it opens the way for moments of synchronicity to happen. Synchronicity, as mentioned before, is when two events happen that aren't normally, or causally, related to each other. The philosopher Plato, and the late Swiss psychiatrist, Carl Jung, developed this theory of synchronicity which literally means "united time"—syn means to unite, and chronos means of time.

So synchronicity is the theory of meaningful co-incidences in which there is no rational causal connection between event A and event

B. But instead there is a symbolic and emotional relationship between the disconnected events.

And so I believe that the sweet synchronicity of finding Annie was for me, a synchronistic event...and one that has taken a book to understand.

Occultists and Jungian psychologists are also aware of the dangers of this process of kriyashakti or active imagination in people who are neurotic or in crisis. The subjective unconscious mind can be left open to negative images that can be disturbing if they are arising from a wounded complex in the psyche. So occultists such as Annie worked hard to train herself to be as clear, conscious and healthy so as not to interfere or awaken personal desires that were not useful or true. That is part of the reason for the warnings against alcohol, drugs, and unhealthy life habits that the esoteric section of the Theosophical Society advocates for its members.

When I used this process of active imagination, or *kriyashakti*, I began to sense that there were a lot of people—not just Annie—on the "other side" who were there for me. They were people I knew who had passed over many years ago, and I found it relaxing to see them in my mind's eye. Sometimes there were fragments of a conversation with them; until my mind wandered. There was, however, a feeling of benevolence and goodness, a lack of judgment, and a sense that the mundane details of this life weren't of such great importance.

I had stopped my astrology readings at the beginning of this writing project, which was wise, because I wouldn't have had the psychic energy to do both. But what was the astrological perspective on all this--outside of the comparison of the two charts in the beginning?

First of all, I believe that Krishnamurti's teachings, with its advocating of living from a place where using *one's free choice* is paramount, can actually be a good balance with astrology. I've always felt that this equation is true: fate + free will = destiny. The fate is what we're born with and what happens to us, but the free will part of the equation is the crucial turning point to how the destiny will be. The astrology chart, based on your time and place of birth, is part of the fate in the equation, but shouldn't be confused with destiny. It's our free will choices (that are sometimes helped by knowing astrology) that make all the difference.

However Krishnamurti would probably have negated astrology in his day, because in India it's used mostly for predictions. There are many astrologers, myself included, that don't stress the predictive part of astrology, but the free will part. And yet, Krishnamurti must have remembered his father saying that the astrologer who drew up his birth chart predicted he would be *a great man*.

In his time astrology was used for prediction, but his teachings were about being unpredictable; free. Yet I believe that creating a balance between the two is possible: we can believe there's an astrological transit or alignment that may influence us, but still we live with our free will choices leading the way.

Annie Besant delved into the hidden worlds of astrology and alchemy, like Carl Jung did, but Annie's path was primarily one of an occultist who looks beneath the appearance of things to what is commonly thought of as "un-seeable." She did that through deep meditation, kriyashakti, yoga, and through her faith in her connection with the Masters. And always, doing service and good work in the world was a priority for her and an absolute requirement for being on the spiritual path.

Her path was one of discipleship to her belief in helping the 'underdog' and the oppressed, and attunement to the "Masters" who guided her. Whereas, Krishnamurti's teachings were about *freedom from discipleship* to any religion, person, path, or conditioned behavior. One can see, from looking at the story of his life, how he would have yearned to be free from roles and expectations that were put upon him—as he often said when he was young:—"why did they have to pick me?"

Astrology, Theosophy and Krishnamurti's teachings are all different facets through which we can look at the world. And when we get beyond the differences and semantics, we see the "perennial philosophy" is in them all: an awareness that one of the highest of virtues is coming from a place of unconditional love and unconditional acceptance. Yes, even astrology promotes compassion for our self and each other. We can see on an astrology chart the wounding, and the sorrows a person has to live with, and feel greater compassion for them—as Henry Wadsworth Longfellow once said: *"If we could read the secret history of our enemies, we would find in each man's life a sorrow and a suffering enough to disarm all hostility."*

It's hard to know what the initial effect of Krishnamurti's rejection of his "Role" had on Annie. It's curious that her opening speech at the last convention was called: "The World Teacher is Here" and yet Krishnamurti was saying exactly the opposite.

In all those years of preparing for the Coming she had begged her readers and listeners to keep an open mind, warning them that what he said might not be acceptable because it would be so new. But now she herself was in danger of falling into the very hole that she had foreshadowed for others. His pronouncements that day and his future talks were so revolutionary that the foundation of her world was rocked, but then she reinvented herself yet again, with her great work in India.

Annie, like all of us, had a public and private persona. In her private letters she shared her worry for the Theosophical Society because she stood in a confusing position. She publicly had said "The Lord is here," and for the Theosophists that meant she must be right, for she was always right to them. Yet Krishnamurti was repudiating the Theosophical path; although doing it rather nicely. Later in life she chose to call herself "his beloved disciple" although in all his talks— and they would continue for the rest of his long life—he said he didn't want disciples.

Annie could be called an *occultist,* in that she looked for what was beneath the surface of things, and she believed in the *evolutionary* journey of the Soul, through the slow process of doing good works, through study and meditation, and the gradual rising of consciousness. Krishnamurti's way was that of the *mystic*—sudden, unexplainable, and needing nothing but an unconditioned and free mind. One could theorize that he achieved that unconditioned state through his suffering in what he called "the process" of his spiritual breakdown and breakthrough as he released the conditioning of his childhood.

The two stances of occultist and mystic aren't easily reconcilable, but Annie still tried to do just that. In her old age, she withdrew more and more from Theosophical activities and leadership in the Society and saw herself as one who was now learning what Krishnamurti had come to teach. It was also in Annie's nature to reinvent herself, and she certainly did that when she poured herself into Indian politics.

Krishnamurti had been raised amid Theosophical beliefs and habits, but the change that came over him during the days before the last few gatherings, through the time of his "breakdown/breakthough process," allowed him to let go of the evolutionary path and leap into a mystical experience where he became One with his Beloved. One can see this change in him after having had that revelation the night he sat under the pepper tree.

From that time on, he had such a profound charisma that he drew crowds and disciples wherever he went. They pressed him to speak and so he did. Many were not happy with what he said, but still, they wanted to learn how to be freer from the troubling conditions of life. They wanted to become unencumbered from their past conditioning so that they could directly experience what he called "freedom from the known" and to connect with "their inner Beloved."

And with his mesmerizing talks he drew thousands of young people to him who knew nothing of Theosophy but who were looking for a way to live, unencumbered by the religious beliefs handed down to them by their parents. In the 1960's and 1970's most people knew who Krishnamurti was, and many people would travel far to hear him speak, and every bookstore in the country carried his books. Today many writers such as Eckart Tolle have drawn heavily on his ideas about living in the "Now"—being present in the moment.

And what about Charles Leadbeater? He stayed within the Society, but often worked in Australia, satisfying his love of ritual and ceremonies by forming the "Liberal Catholic Church" and appointing himself as Bishop. He wrote many excellent books such as: "The Chakras" and the compassionate: "For Those Who Grieve" yet he has always aroused controversy. In occult circles, many people regard him as an unparalleled clairvoyant who could see into the hidden energy centers in the body—his book on the chakras has been a best-seller ever since he wrote it. He understood the yogic kundalini experience and could clairvoyantly read past lives through the 'Akashic reords.' He delved deeply into occult chemistry. There was no doubt that he was a brilliant and gifted writer.

Yet many people still see Leadbeater as a black magician and pedophile. Newspapers in

Australia, where Leadbeater spent most of his time, alleged that he either taught his students masturbation or he touched them, and they encouraged the police to investigate.

Leadbeater was a person of tremendous intelligence, imagination and power combined with tremendous panache—and yet perhaps—it could have been part of a dissociated personality. One part of him may not have known what the other part did. According to one book: *The Elder Brother,* by Gregory Tillett, he was a totally self-created man who imaginatively construed the history of his life, even changing his birth year and place so that people would not be able to know of his humble origins or trace his life story. He invented himself as he so desired, and we may never know his deepest secrets or if he had a dissociated personality.

Annie was a person of great loyalty—a person who having once given her loyalty to someone or something has a hard time changing that position, yet her greatest loyalty was to truth. Annie never doubted Krishnamurti, but it pained her greatly to doubt Charles Leadbeater, as she did when she feared his sexual influence on Krishnamurti. She later understood the situation less radically, when she learned that teaching masturbation was an ancient Greek practice among teachers and pupils, and was done to help the students not be distracted by sexual affairs. And so she "conditionally" allowed him back into the Society although he wasn't Krishnamurti's tutor any more. At that time, Annie, and most Theosophists, believed that Charles was not a pedophile as he acted as a meticulous Victorian gentleman, although according to Tillett, in *The Elder Brother*, there is now much evidence to prove that he was just that. Today Theosophists seem to take what was good of what he taught and wrote, and leave the rest to the historians.

The Swiss psychologist, Carl Jung, once said that it was the wise person who could hold and contain the tension of the opposites within themselves, and this, I believe, was what Annie was incredibly gifted at doing. She was forced to struggle with her beliefs and her loyalty to her mother, to Bradlaugh, to Shaw, to Madame, to Charles, and to Krishnamurti. But Annie never lost her deep love for each of these people, and it is interesting to note that Krishnamurti never changed in his love for her and Leadbeater died less than 6 months after Annie died. Annie could always see both sides of a situation or a person, and in many ways she succeeded in bringing forth their best potential.

Annie was a classic Libra, in that she saw both sides of an issue or situation, and always sought reconciliation. Her warrior-like Aries Rising gave her the strength to make decisions and to create ever new reforms and ways to make the world a better place.

Without Annie, women and children would have suffered longer in poor paying jobs in factories, and without knowledge of birth control. Children, and especially girls, would not have had the educational opportunities and for the poorest, the chance to eat food at school. The Theosophical Society as it is would not exist today, nor would we have the teachings of Krishnamurti. And without her tireless campaigning for home rule in India, it would have been doubtful if the Indians would have been ready for Gandhi and Nehru's leadership.

And last, what of the astrological connections between Annie and I that were mentioned in the first chapter? For those who are interested, I'll touch on a few more observations. Annie was born Oct. 1st 1847 at 5:39 pm outside of London, England, and I was born Oct. 1st 1947 at 5:34 pm outside of Hartford, Connecticut, in the U.S.

As mentioned in the beginning, we're both Libras, with Aries rising, and we each have a T-square suggesting the kind of inner pressure that causes one to take action in the outer world. The T-squares for both of us, have a focal planet in the 4th house of home, and primarily involve Mercury, Mars, Moon, and Uranus. The

T-squares are motivating influences, and for us they particularly effect our emotions and the need to express what we believe.

Our Sun signs, (the Sun representing the Self) are at 7 degrees of Libra, in the 7th house of relationships. One very well respected astrology program that compared our two charts writes about this synastry: *"You are likely to feel an almost telepathic connection with each other. There is a deeper purpose to your connection that you each seek to bring out."* Libra holds the tension of opposites, as it's the sign of the scales, and seeks equality, justice and harmony.

Again, looking at my chart, my future oriented North Node is in the sign of Taurus, with the past-life oriented South Node being in the sign of Scorpio, reflecting a past of considerable trauma, drama, rebirth and regeneration. This South Node is accentuated by being conjunct Jupiter, which enhances the idea of my past life having been a large one of much drama, perhaps being a person "behind the throne." Annie was often in that position as well. My Taurus North Node implies that the reincarnatin Soul in this life seeks serenity rather than larger than life drama, and needs ways "to find God in the simple beautiful things" in this life. It needs to feel that life can be safe and uncomplicated again.

In comparing the two charts we see that my Mercury is opposite Annie's Pluto, indicating that *"one person may seek to plumb the depths of the other's psyche. Communication between you two is with the intent of exploring the Unknown."*

My Venus is conjunct Annie's Mercury, my Moon is quintile to Annie's Moon, and we both have our Moons trine to Saturn*: "a sense of creative commitment to mutual goals and a sense of loyalty."*

What is quite *different* between our charts is that Annie has Uranus conjuncting Pluto and close to Mars, all in her first house. This would describe a person who is active (Mars) and revolutionary (Uranus) and attuned to the occult (Pluto). There is an intensity here that is modified by her Moon conjuncting Jupiter in the nurturing sign of Cancer. When reflecting on Annie's passionate reforming-activist qualities we can see this easily. And we see the strong influence of the mother and perhaps the lack of mother love in the Moon/Jupiter conjunction in the 4th house squaring Uranus on one side and Venus on the other side—her t-square.

And in my chart, the mother/nurturing issue is reflected in Moon in Aries square to Mars in Leo, and my love of spirituality, the occult and the mystical is reflected in my 3 planet-stellium of Sun conjuncting Neptune, conjuncting Venus.

And finally, my Moon conjuncts Annie's Pluto: *"You may be coming together to do some serious healing. There may be a feeling of being together for some karmic purpose. There is a serious soul-purpose bringing you together—there may be walled off feelings of pain and anger from early childhood perhaps going back to issues with mother love or its lack, that come to light in the course of this relationship."* Did we also come together to heal or nurture each other in some way? Could I have been her mother? Could I have been her? Why have I spent over 7 years writing about her? I'm not sure there's a knowable answer to these questions; I think much is meant to remain a mystery.

For those who are interested in J. Krishnamurti's chart, he was born on May 12th, 1895 at 12:30 am, in Madanapalle, India. What is most interesting in his chart is the strong presence of the planet, Uranus, a planetary archetype that represents our urge for individuality, freedom, and the high likelihood that "the unexpected" will be a repeating pattern in one's life.

Astrologically there is always more one could say, and each astrologer would probably notice different things. But I wanted to give the reader who has some knowledge of astrology a glimpse into our charts, because that is what first caught my eye and started this journey.

I believe Annie and I worked together to tell this story—that I couldn't have written this book without her—and that my obsessiveness with her life story came from this connection. The book has been collaboration. She has quickened my belief in my inner Self, Atman, or 'Master' and the accessibility of people on the other side who have passed over, through *kriyashakti: using the power of thought to manifest things on the physical plane.*

And to all the readers, I hope this has stimulated your curiosity and sense of awe and mystery! It certainly has done that for me.

If you have any comments or questions on this book, you may contact me through: elizabethspring@aol.com or learn more about my work and other books at: www.elizabethspring.com. If you wish to buy more copies, the book is easily available through www.amazon.com

Made in the USA
Charleston, SC
21 February 2015